T0327939

KONBINI

コンビニ

KONBINI

コンビニ

Cult recipes, stories and adventures
from Japan's iconic convenience stores

Brendan Liew
Caryn Ng

Smith
Street
Books

Contents

目次

Introduction 09
Cook's Notes 13

1 Onigiri 16
Onigiri: A love story 19
Konbini: In the beginning 33
Seasonal delights 42

2 The hot snacks counter 44
Konbini today 57
The cult of Karaage-Kun 69

3 Osouzai 84
Konbini arenji & Kushiyaki 96
Social infrastructure 107

4 Bento: More than rice 128
Konbini greetings 130
From the Konbini shelves 162

5 Bakery 165
The premium roll cake 180
Going local 195
Avatars, deep-freeze technology
 & konbinis of the future 201
Behind the Konbini: A chat with Lawson 215

6 Desserts 218
Final reflections 241

Basics 244
Glossary 246
Index 249
Thanks 254

Introduction

GREY CLOUDS ARE GATHERING OVERHEAD in the remote area of Tohoku, in the eastern part of the main island of Honshu. We'd just stepped off the Shinkansen at the near-deserted station, our destination a 600-year-old ryokan accessible only via shuttle bus.

The shuttle bus sets off, making its way through winding, wild forest roads and terraced fields of pale green rice, their tops laden with ripe, golden husks. For the last stretch up to the ryokan, we are ushered to a car to take us up a steep, one-lane narrow slope.

This onsen town is surrounded by mountains and covered with fog and mist. A few ryokans are clustered here, around a hot spring source once frequented by the great damiyō (feudal lord), Date Masamune. The staff stay in lodgings a short walk away, and a local bus services the area every three hours. Aside from the ryokans and a new small, chic cafe, there is nothing else.

We pass an ancient wood and glass stall with a traditional wooden sign reading 'vegetable store' written in calligraphic kanji. It is closed, the plaster walls bare, though the two wooden tables inside where vegetables were once displayed are polished and clean, gleaming gently in the light.

Over dinner, we ask the young ryokan attendant how she finds living here. 'It is difficult,' she admits. 'There is no konbini, no transport, and the bus to the nearest city runs infrequently.'

We found it intriguing that the first thing the ryokan attendant mentioned was the absence of a konbini – a sign, perhaps, of how entrenched in Japanese culture the convenience store has become.

In 2023, the konbini commemorated 50 years in Japan, from the single humble 7-Eleven store in Toyosu (though Family Mart actually opened in Saitama a year earlier), to the tens of thousands of konbinis that have now taken hold in the cities and prefectures. In the dense heart of Tokyo, the familiar glow of the konbini's lights – the green, blue and white of Famima (Family Mart); the orange, red and green of Sebun (7-Eleven); and the blue, white and pink of Lawson – can be glimpsed down the narrow laneways and around the corners of the high-rise concrete blocks.

They camouflage themselves among the neon lights of izakayas and bars on neighbourhood streets, and in the more traditional areas, such as Kyoto, where the Miyagi Landscape Guidelines – strict rules to preserve the historical aesthetics of the city – apply, they blend in with the ancient capital, their signs altered to calm, subdued tones.

Konbinis, in the foreign psyche, are an almost mystical world, quite unlike any other – which might explain the occasionally dazed gaikokujin (foreigner) spotted slowly wandering through the aisles.

The impeccable perfection of the display; the sheer variety of intriguing and exotic-looking products; the food... It's all so intrinsically Japanese: Japanese chocolates, snacks, breads, desserts. There's karaage, daifuku, dango, and depending on the time of the year, tsukimi keki (moon-viewing cakes; traditionally seen in September) and oden (fishcakes braised in dashi in autumn and winter). There's the manga section, the cooling patches to stick on when you have a fever, the anime characters on and in packaging...

To the locals, konbinis have become part of their 'life infrastructure' (an official classification by the Japanese government). And in small towns like the one we visited, whose humble attractions or onsens may have faded from their historic Taishō, Edo or Shōwa glory days, the konbini – or its absence – is keenly felt.

The depopulation of Japan's towns – the shuttering of shopping strips, and disappearance of small shops like the Taisho-era vegetable stall we chanced across, which in ancient days may have proudly sold plump eggplants (aubergines), leafy vegetables, delicious starchy sato-imo (local yams) and other local produce – has made resources such as the konbini more valuable than ever.

Whether you've lived in Tokyo, where a konbini is but a block away, or the outskirts, where you've pulled up to a konbini parking lot sometime in the day or night. Whether you've dashed inside in summer for some aisu (ice cream) or electrolyte-replenishing chilled litchi with Okinawa sea salt juice, or in winter for a karaage or konnyaku to escape the cold. Whether you've picked up a quick onigiri in the morning before a train journey, or tried some exotic snack for the sheer fun – this book is for you.

Alongside our travel stories and interviews with Lawson (that of the blue, white and pink stripes), we hope our collection of konbini recipes – from the playful to the proper – gives you an authentic taste and deeper insight into how the konbini has become part of life in this corner of the world.

Cook's notes

FOR THIS BOOK, WE WANTED to cover one of our favourite Japanese haunts – the konbini, which is such a large part of everyday life in Japan. To date, we've uncovered Tokyo in a day (*Tokyo Local*; *A Day in Tokyo*) and the izakayas, makanai (staff meals) and late-night dishes that define Tokyo at night (*Tokyo Up Late*).

This book is an ode to all who live outside Japan and miss konbini, and a welcome to those who have yet to step inside this 'B-gourmet' wonderland of legendary repute ('B-gourmet' referring to inexpensive but nostalgic and popular dishes).

While our previous books focused on recipes and restaurant dishes that are accessible – and also, if desired, a challenge (making your own ramen noodles from scratch, for instance) – here we hone in on items you can find in the aisles, shelves and freezer sections of a Japanese konbini. These are dishes both nostalgic and simple, easily put together for weeknight meals – but with techniques and tips from a chef with a Japanese culinary background.

These konbini favourites are the dishes that sustain Japan. The simple, after-work pleasures. The lunch-time rush, and the early-morning onigiri or bakery pick-me-up. The exotic yōshoku (Western-style) hybrids, and the increasing influence of Indian (curries), Chinese and Korean food on Japanese palates. We've added twists and suggested variations, though this is but a slice of what a konbini has to offer!

We hope you enjoy this book and the stories behind the konbini, made possible through interviews and a visit to Lawson's headquarters in Tokyo (Dōmo arigatou gozaimasu Lawson and Mochimaru Ken-san).

Ingredient notes

As fruit and vegetables come in all shapes and sizes, here is a guide to the weight of common vegetables used in the recipes:

+ onion 150 g (5½ oz)

+ potato 150 g (5½ oz)

+ carrot 150 g (5½ oz)

Unless specified, all fruits and vegetables are medium sized.

+ Butter is unsalted.

+ Eggs are 60 g (2 oz).

+ Cream is whipping cream.

+ Flour is plain (all-purpose), unless otherwise stated.

+ Salt is fine sea salt, unless otherwise stated.

+ Pepper is freshly ground black pepper, unless otherwise stated.

+ Sugar is white caster (superfine) sugar, unless otherwise specified.

+ Sake is cooking sake, not drinking sake.

+ Soy sauce is koikuchi (Japanese dark soy sauce), unless otherwise stated. We suggest using a low-sodium variety. This gives you more opportunity to adjust the salt levels to your taste.

+ For a neutral-flavoured oil, we suggest rice bran as it's flavourless and has a high smoke point, so it's less likely to impart a burnt taste to your food when stir-frying. To prolong the life of the oil after deep-frying, let it cool, then filter it using paper towels, and store in the container it came in. It can be reused until the taste becomes pronounced or it turns nut brown.

Worcestershire sauce, chunou sauce, tonkatsu sauce and okonomiyaki sauce: what's the difference?

Worcestershire sauce

ウスターソース

In Japan, worcestershire sauce is thicker than its Western counterparts. Made from vegetables and fruits, it has a mild sourness, sweetness and spiciness. It lies somewhere between a Western worcestershire and a barbecue sauce.

Chunou sauce

中濃ソース

The sauce sits between tonkatsu sauce and worcestershire sauce, with a medium body and flavour. Like worcestershire sauce, it is used as an ingredient in cooking.

Tonkatsu sauce

とんかつソース

Containing many fruits and with a strong sweet and sour flavour, tonkatsu sauce is thicker than worcestershire sauce and chunou sauce. It is mostly served as a finished sauce on dishes.

Okonomiyaki sauce

お好み焼きソース

More akin to chunou sauce in flavour and consistency, okonomiyaki sauce is less spicy and less thick than tonkatsu sauce. If you can't find it, you can substitute either chunou sauce or tonkatsu sauce in a pinch, adding 1 tablespoon oyster sauce for every 3 tablespoons chunou or tonkatsu sauce.

1 Onigiri

おにぎり

Onigiri/Omusibi   20

Rice mix-ins   22

Shio salmon   25

Okaka (bonito flakes)   25

Awase miso   29

Gochujang chicken   29

Makizushi   34

Negitoro   38

Onigiri, or omusubi, is Japan's original convenience food: rice (plain, sometimes grilled), packed around a delicious filling, with nori as a finishing touch. A popular bento item from school children's picnics to office workers' lunchboxes and hanami (cherry blossom) gatherings, onigiri were also the starting point for the konbini wave that swept across Japan. Without this humble rice ball, konbinis may not be the phenomenon they are today.

It would be remiss to start a book on konbinis with anything other than onigiri – the item that continues to be the anytime snack, from morning to late night, on Shinkansen trips, hikes and holidays.

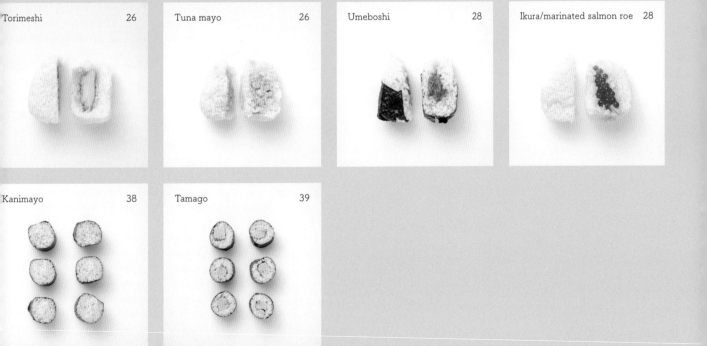

| Torimeshi | 26 | Tuna mayo | 26 | Umeboshi | 28 | Ikura/marinated salmon roe | 28 |

| Kanimayo | 38 | Tamago | 39 |

Onigiri: A love story

FIRST SEEN IN JAPAN AS CHIMAKI – glutinous rice wrapped in bamboo leaves – onigiri have appeared throughout history from as far back as the royal court (the writings of Lady Murasaki in 973–1020) to samurai battlefields in the 17th century. It's even immortalised by Studio Ghibli: Haku gives it to Chihiro in the garden of Yubaba's sento to comfort and nourish her in *Spirited Away*.

The onigiri – a familiar, even quintessential, symbol of Japanese cuisine – was the one thing that set the konbini on its path of 'wa' (Japanese-ness) and secured its future. Five years after the first konbini opened its doors, the concept had yet to be fully accepted, and it wasn't until 7-Eleven decided to sell onigiri at its stores that the konbini began to be truly embraced.

7-Eleven might have brought onigiri to the konbini, but it is Lawson that introduced a premium range of onigiri in 2002. Packed in snazzy black with alluring photos of the fillings on the cover, this Rolls-Royce offering of the onigiri world focuses on local ingredients: maguro tataki with egg yolk and shiso seeds, plump whole premium umeboshi made with nanko ume, grilled salmon, pearls of ikura marinated in shoyu...

Then, there's Lawson's starkly minimalist onigiri from the Okomeguri series, displayed in all its pure, naked glory: a perfectly formed triangular rice ball mixed with nothing but salt. It's designed to showcase the rice – in this case, rice grown in different prefectures across Japan – and introduce these to a broader audience: instead of committing to buying a small bag of raw rice from Yamagata or Ishikawa, why not have a taste through an onigiri first?

Onigiri / Omusubi

おにぎり・お結び

At its simplest a plain rice ball, hand-pressed into a triangular shape and wrapped with a sheath of nori, onigiri is a beloved comfort food – conjuring up memories of okāsan (mothers) preparing it in their kitchens for their children.

Onigiri, or omusubi – the latter referring to the mountain shape the rice is moulded into – is the humble Japanese item that spurred on the konbini's popularity. The myriad flavours it comes in make it a top-selling item.

For those of us living outside Japan, where a konbini isn't an easy stroll away, onigiri are fortunately a dish that can be easily prepared at home. The recipes that follow are a small slice of the many flavours you can find in konbini.

You can also enjoy onigiri grilled (yaki onigiri): lightly butter a pan and fry the onigiri on both sides to create a crisp crust on the exterior, then brush lightly with soy sauce.

Cooking the rice

300 g (10½ oz) uncooked white sushi (short-grain) rice
320 ml (11 fl oz) water

1. Wash the rice in a colander until the water runs clear; you'll need about 3–4 changes of water. Soak the rice for 1 hour in a fresh bowl of water, then drain the rice again.

2. Place the rice and water in a rice cooker and cook as directed by the manufacturer. Alternatively, place in a saucepan, put the lid on, bring to the boil, turn the heat to low for 10 minutes, then allow to rest for 15 minutes. The actual time and water quantity needed may vary depending on the brand or batch of rice you use, so experiment to achieve the perfect rice. If the rice is too hard or dry, add a little more water; if it's too moist, remove a little water, or reduce the resting time.

3. While the rice is still warm, shape as directed below.

Shaping the rice

600 g (1 lb 5 oz) warm cooked sushi rice (from above)
6 teaspoons rice mix-ins (optional, see page 23)
250 ml (1 cup) water
1 tablespoon salt
6 tablespoons fillings of your choice (see pages 24–31)
2 nori sheets, each cut into 3 rectangles

1. Mix your rice gently with any mix-ins, if using, then drape a damp, clean cloth over your rice to keep it moist and warm while you shape the onigiri.

2. Mix together the water and salt and place next to your rice.

3. Using clean hands, dip your hands into the salt water, then divide the rice into six portions. Working with one portion at a time, and keeping the rest covered, flatten one piece, place a tablespoon of filling in the centre, then encase the filling with rice.

4. Press the rice firmly but gently into a circle or triangle, dipping your hands into the salt water if the rice is sticking. Wrap the onigiri in a piece of nori.

5. Repeat with the remaining ingredients to make six onigiri. Wrap in plastic wrap, or place in an airtight container and refrigerate. They will keep fresh for up to 18 hours.

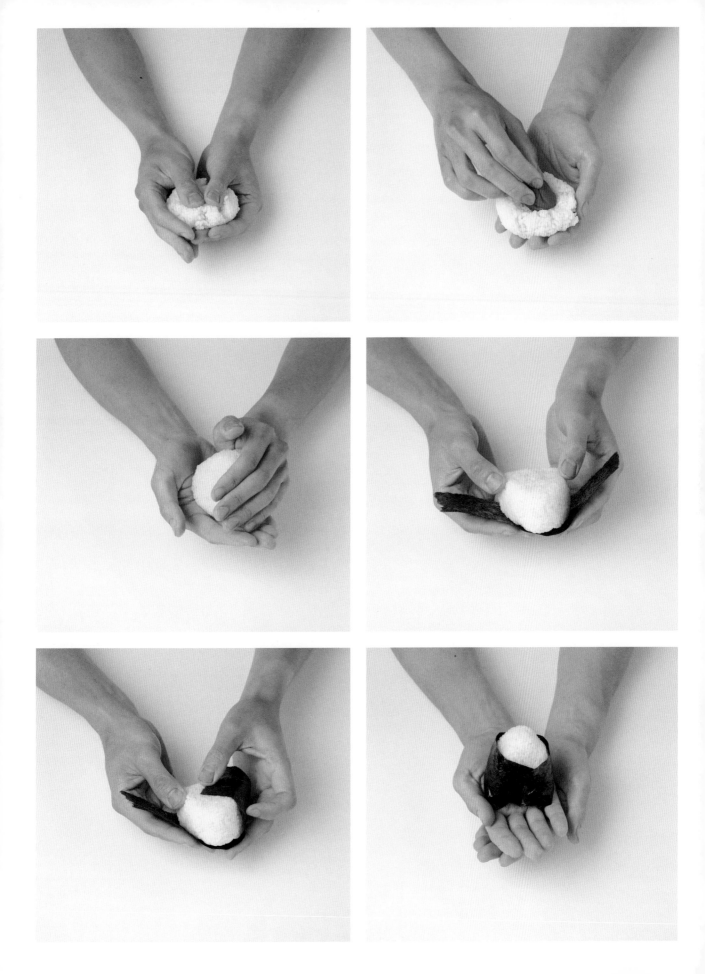

Rice mix-ins

Adding other ingredients to the rice creates textures and flavours that complement the filling, and make a plain omusubi more interesting. Add as much or as little as you like, but as a guide, roughly 1 teaspoon per onigiri works well.

Chirimen sansho

Chirimen are tiny, roasted fish; sansho is a dried berry, similar to Chinese sichuan peppercorns. They are often combined and served with rice. Chirimen has a nice chewy texture and fish flavour, while the sansho is a little spicy and numbing, balancing the oceanic taste. You may find this mixture in the furikake (rice topping) section of Asian and Japanese grocers. If you can't find chirimen, you can substitute dried small baby anchovies, pan toasted with a small amount of cracked toasted sichuan pepper.

Furikake

The simplest rice addition is store-bought furikake. These fun, dried rice seasonings come in many different ingredient combinations. A small amount added to omusubi can change the flavour and texture considerably.

Shiso & sesame

Shred a few shiso leaves and mix with roasted sesame seeds to imbue the rice with the refreshing flavour of shiso and the roasted nutty taste of sesame.

Tsukudani

Tsukudani is made by braising sliced kombu (or mushrooms) in a sauce strongly flavoured with soy. You may be able to find it in your Asian and Japanese grocer. Drain off the excess liquid, then add to the rice for a strong umami flavour.

Wakame

Wakame gives the rice a great texture. If using dried wakame, soak about 1–2 tablespoons in cold water until hydrated (about 20 minutes). When soft, drain thoroughly, roughly chop into small pieces and mix with the rice.

Yukari

A blend of dried shiso and umeboshi (pickled plum) adds a pleasant pink colour and refreshing salty–tart flavour to the onigiri. Yukari can be found in Asian and Japanese grocers. Only add half a teaspoon per onigiri for the effect.

Furikake
ふりかけ

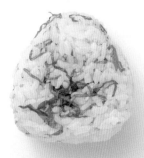

Shiso & sesame
しそごま

Tsukudani
佃煮

Wakame
ワカメ

Yukari
ゆかり

Onigiri fillings

Most of these 'fillings' (except the tuna mayo version) can be served over rice as a main meal. A great idea is to make one of these simple dishes for dinner, but prepare more than you need, and cook up extra rice as well, so you can shape the left-over rice and filling into onigiri balls, wrap them, and keep them in the fridge overnight for lunch the next day.

Each filling will make enough for 6 onigiri, or serve 1 person as a main meal if dished over rice.

Shio salmon
塩鮭

Shio salmon (alternative)
塩鮭

Okaka
おかか

Shio salmon

塩鮭

The classic of salt and salmon flakes with a hint of sake.

Mentsuyu
30 g (1 oz) salt
30 ml (1 fl oz) sake
300 ml (10 fl oz) cold water
300 g (10½ oz) salmon fillet, skin on

1. In a bowl, mix together the salt, sake and water until the salt has dissolved. Place the salmon fillet in and marinate for 15 minutes.

2. Remove the salmon from the liquid and pat dry. Place on a plate, skin side up, and leave uncovered in the refrigerator for 8 hours, or overnight.

3. When you're ready to cook, heat an oven grill (broiler) to high. Cook the salmon, skin side up, for 5–6 minutes (depending on the thickness of the fish), until the meat flakes easily and the skin is crispy.

4. Allow to cool, then flake the salmon flesh into a bowl. Shred the crispy skin and mix it through the salmon, then use the mixture to fill your onigiri (page 20). Alternatively, cut the flesh into chunks, place on your onigiri, along with a piece of crispy skin, and wrap in nori.

Okaka (bonito flakes)

おかか

A simple, delicious filling of katsuobushi that have been mixed with a soy-based broth. This recipe is a good way of using katsuobushi already steeped for making dashi.

6 tablespoons katsuobushi (bonito flakes; see note)
2 tablespoons mentsuyu (see below)

Mentsuyu
40 ml (1¼ fl oz) mirin
2 teaspoons sugar
100 ml (3½ fl oz) soy sauce
2 cm (¾ inch) square of kombu

1. First, make the mentsuyu. Pour the mirin into a small saucepan and bring to the boil, taking care as the mirin may catch fire. After boiling for a minute, turn the heat to low and add the sugar. Cook, stirring, until dissolved.

2. Add the remaining mentsuyu ingredients and bring to a simmer. Simmer over very low heat (it should barely be bubbling) for 5 minutes.

3. Strain out the kombu, reserving the liquid. This liquid is your mentsuyu; it can be stored in the refrigerator for up to a week and added to dashi for a quick noodle broth.

4. Mix 2 tablespoons of the mentsuyu with the 6 tablespoons of katsuobushi and use this mixture to stuff your omusubi (page 20).

Note
You can also use katsuobushi reserved from making dashi (page 245). Place it in a non-stick frying pan and cook over medium–low heat to dry the flakes. When mostly dry, place in a small bowl, mix with 2 tablespoons of mentsuyu from above and use to stuff your omusubi.

Torimeshi

とりめし

While commonly associated with Japanese cuisine, teriyaki chicken is not actually common in Japan. What you'll find in Japan instead is torimeshi – chicken cooked in a sweet and aromatic thickened sauce which can be served over rice or in onigiri. The sauce in torimeshi onigiri flavours the rice, and the nugget of succulent chicken in the centre is a nice surprise.

1 boneless chicken thigh (about 200 g/7 oz), skin off
salt
2 tablespoons neutral-flavoured oil
1 tablespoon water
1 tablespoon soy sauce
1 tablespoon mirin
1 tablespoon sake
1 teaspoon sugar
½ teaspoon potato starch

1. Pierce the chicken thigh with a fork and sprinkle all over with salt. Heat a frying pan over medium–high heat, then add the oil. Sear the chicken on all sides, until well coloured.

2. Meanwhile, in a small bowl, mix together the remaining ingredients.

3. Pour the soy sauce mixture into the frying pan with the chicken – be careful as it may splatter. Turn the heat down low and continue cooking, basting the chicken with the liquid, until the chicken is fully cooked; this should take about 6 minutes in total.

4. Remove the chicken and sauce to a plate and allow to cool. Cut the chicken into bite-sized pieces and use to stuff your omusubi (page 20), drizzling each with a little of the sauce.

Tuna mayo

ツナマヨ

One of the oldest and best selling onigiri is tuna mayo. The combination of creamy mayo (preferably Kewpie) with the subtle, oceanic flavour of tuna and the crunch and sweetness of corn is beloved by all. This is a staple of lunchboxes across Japan.

185 g (6½ oz) tin of tuna in brine
60 g (¼ cup) mayonnaise
1 tablespoon soy sauce
2–3 tablespoons cooked corn (optional)

1. Drain the tuna thoroughly, then mix with the remaining ingredients, breaking the tuna into small pieces.

2. Place inside or on top of your omusubi (page 20) for a simple, classic and delicious konbini staple.

Torimeshi
とりめし

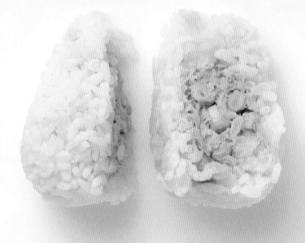

Tuna mayo
ツナマヨ

Umeboshi (pickled plum)

梅干し

The simplest omusubi filling, but a Japanese favourite. If you can, use a good-quality umeboshi from your local Asian or Japanese grocer. Lawson uses the prized nanko ume in its premium umeboshi range. The tartness of the umeboshi makes this a nice addition to a bento containing other richer onigiri.

6 pieces umeboshi (pickled plum)

1. Simply place the plum pieces inside or on top of your onigiri (page 20).

2. If the plum still has the seed inside, let the diner know, so they don't accidentally swallow the seed!

Ikura/marinated salmon roe

イクラ

A luxe onigiri with briny pops of marinated salmon roe.

20 ml (¾ fl oz) sake
25 ml (1 fl oz) mirin
25 ml (1 fl oz) usukuchi soy sauce
50 g (1¾ oz) salmon roe

1. Pour the sake and mirin into a small pot and bring to the boil. Allow to boil for 30 seconds, then take off the heat and pour in the soy sauce. Chill in the refrigerator until cold.

2. Place the salmon roe in a colander and gently rinse with cold water, replacing the water three times. Drain thoroughly and pick out any pearls of roe that have burst.

3. When the soy mixture is cold, add the salmon roe. Cover and marinate in the fridge for 3 hours.

4. Drain the salmon roe, discarding the soy mixture, and use to stuff your onigiri (page 20). Any left-over roe can be refrigerated in an airtight container for up to 3 days.

Additional filling options:
Fried chicken (page 70)
Shigureni (page 80)
Black vinegar–braised pork belly & marinated eggs (page 86)
Sanma kabayaki, shredded (page 92)

Awase miso

合わせ味噌

A thick sauce with the richness of miso to spread over onigiri before grilling. The miso provides a salty, complex and toasty flavour to onigiri.

1 tablespoon white miso
1 tablespoon hatcho or red miso
1 tablespoon saikyo miso
1½ teaspoons mirin

1. Mix all the ingredients together, taste, then add more saikyo miso for sweetness or red miso for saltiness, to suit your taste.

2. Make your omusubi (page 20), then smear a layer of miso on top. Grill (broil) until darkened, then wrap with nori and enjoy.

Gochujang chicken

コチュジャンチキン

Korean flavours are enjoying rising popularity in Japan. This chicken filling gives a spicier, richer kind of torimeshi due to the addition of Korean gochujang – a fermented red chilli paste. The karaage chicken coating absorbs the sauce, packing more flavour into each bite.

1 tablespoon roasted sesame seeds
1 tablespoon gochujang
1½ teaspoons ketchup
1 teaspoon oyster sauce
6 pieces karaage chicken (page 76), cold, cut into bite-sized pieces
1 shiso leaf, finely shredded

Mix together the sesame seeds, gochujang, ketchup and oyster sauce. Add the chicken and shiso, then use to stuff your omusubi (page 20).

Umeboshi

梅干し

Ikura

イクラ

Awase miso
合わせ味噌

Gochujang chicken
コチュジャンチキン

Konbini: In the beginning

THE CONVENIENCE STORE TRACES its roots back to North America, where 7-Eleven and Lawson came about. In the case of Lawson, we need to go back to Ohio of 1939, where dairy plant owner, J.J. Lawson, decided to create a small store – a milk bar – where locals could come by to pick up fresh, creamy milk each morning. The range expanded to include eggs and orange juice, and by 1970, Lawson's Milk Company had grown to hundreds of locations throughout America.

In 1975, they made the leap across the Pacific Ocean to Japan, partnering with Japanese supermarket brand Daiei to bring Lawson – and the idea of the convenience store – to the Land of the Rising Sun.

As with Western cuisine (yōshoku) and many other foreign influences, Japan took the convenience store and made it her own – though this wasn't the case to begin with. The very first konbini on Japanese shores (a 7-Eleven, brought over by Japanese department store chain Ito-Yokado in 1973) adopted the American format, while Lawson's first store sold 'American foods with a party theme'.

It wasn't until five years later, when 7-Eleven began introducing onigiri instead of serving hot dogs, that the konbini would come to be looked at more favourably. Everyone's favourite Heian-era rice ball would prove to be the tide-turner, pulling more Japanese products onto konbini shelves. Traces of Americana still linger in konbinis, however, with the America Dog or Big America Dog (corn dog) sold alongside yakitori, Family Mart's famous Famichiki (a fried chicken steak which proudly declares on its paper wrapper 'I am Chicken'), and Lawson's just-as-famous chicken nuggets, Karaage-Kun.

Makizushi

巻き寿司

For the rice
30 ml (1 fl oz) rice vinegar
1½ teaspoons sugar
2 teaspoons salt
280–360 g (10–12½ oz) warm
    cooked sushi rice (page 20)
2 nori sheets

Makizushi are rolled sushi, found next to the omusubi in konbinis. Any of the following rolls can be made healthier and with more filling by including some cucumber, avocado, shiso leaf, blanched spinach, shredded carrot, lettuce, natto or mentaiko.

In a small bowl, whisk together the rice vinegar, sugar and salt until dissolved. Pour over the sushi rice and, using a spatula, fold the vinegar into the rice, being careful not to break up the rice. Place a damp cloth over the top to keep the rice warm and stop it drying out.

Shaping the rolls

1. Nori normally comes marked with lines going across the sheet.

2. To make a chūmaki (medium-sized roll), cut about one-third off the top of the sheet for each roll, and use 120–140 g (4½–5 oz) of rice per roll. Spread the rice out over the nori, leaving a 1.5 cm (½ inch) border free from rice at the top. Place about 2 tablespoons or 50 g (1¾ oz) of your chosen filling (see pages 38–41) across the centre of the nori. Dampen the uncovered nori edge with a little water to help the roll stick together, then tightly roll up from the bottom, encasing the filling with the rice and nori.

3. For a futomaki (large sushi roll), leave the sheet uncut and use 160–180 g (5½–6½ oz) of rice per roll.

Ehōmaki
恵方巻

Once a year, konbinis roll out large ehōmaki, an oversized, uncut sushi roll enjoyed only on Setsubun (節分) – the day before the beginning of spring (start of February), where the tradition is to eat the ehōmaki silently in that year's lucky direction. Keeping the rolls uncut ensures you are not 'cutting' your fortune heading into the new year.

As with Japan's many other seasonal festivals, konbinis are quick to partake in the celebrations, being convenient places to buy the lucky item.

Traditionally, ehōmaki contained ingredients such as braised sea eel, braised gourd, crab and tamago. They now come in a variety of fillings, with particularly luxe versions containing wagyu beef, tuna belly and lobster. There are even dessert ehōmaki, in the form of fruit-filled mini roll cakes.

Negitoro

ネギトロ

A Japanese favourite of sashimi-grade tuna with spring onion and a dash of mayonnaise. This filling should be used the same day.

2 tablespoons mirin
2 tablespoons soy sauce
100 g (3½ oz) sashimi-grade raw tuna, chopped
1½ teaspoons mayonnaise
½ teaspoon instant dashi powder
1 tablespoon finely sliced spring onion (scallion)

1. Boil the mirin in a small saucepan for 1 minute, then turn off the heat. Stir in the soy sauce and allow to cool.

2. Mix the tuna with the mayonnaise and dashi powder, then add 1 tablespoon of the soy mixture, adding more soy sauce or mayo to taste. Finally, mix in the spring onion gently, so as to not bruise the spring onion.

Kanimayo

カニマヨ

In this makizushi, the addition of kanimiso (crab guts found in the shell; a coveted part of the crab in Japan) brings a nice savoury earthiness to the sweet crab flesh. This filling is best enjoyed within 18 hours.

100 g (3½ oz) cooked crabmeat
1 tablespoon mayonnaise
½ teaspoon kanimiso (optional)
1 teaspoon roasted sesame seeds

Drain any excess liquid from the crab. Mix the crab with the remaining ingredients.

Tamago

たまご

4 eggs
120 ml (4 fl oz) Dashi
  (page 245)
2 teaspoons mirin
1 teaspoon soy sauce
pinch of salt
1 teaspoon potato starch
2 tablespoons neutral-flavoured oil

A sweet egg omelette is a classic makizushi (rolled sushi) ingredient. It can be added to almost any makizushi filling, or simply used on its own, as in this recipe. The slight sweetness of the omelette (from the mirin) provides a nice contrast to the nori and rice. You can also add julienned cucumber and slices of avocado for freshness, crunch and creaminess.

1. Whisk or blend together the eggs, dashi, mirin, soy sauce and salt.

2. Place the potato starch in a bowl. Strain about 60 ml (¼ cup) of the egg mixture into the potato starch and whisk until uniform. Strain in the remaining egg mixture and whisk until smooth and no streaks of egg yolk or white are visible.

3. Heat a frying pan over medium heat and add the oil. Swirl the oil around to coat the pan, then pour the oil from the pan into a small bowl and reserve.

4. Pour one-third of the egg mixture into the pan and swirl to evenly coat the pan. Using chopsticks, puncture any large air bubbles to create a mostly flat surface.

5. When the egg mixture is mostly set (the egg doesn't flow freely if you pick up the pan and gently swirl it), begin rolling the egg over, starting from the side furthest away from you and rolling towards you. You should have a squarish, roll-shaped omelette.

6. Using chopsticks, dip a piece of paper towel into the reserved oil and use that to grease the empty side of the pan. Push the omelette to the side of the pan furthest from you and grease where the omelette previously was.

7. Pour in another one-third of the egg mixture and swirl it around the pan, lifting the omelette so the raw egg goes under it, sticking the new egg to the omelette. This also prevents the omelette getting too browned underneath.

8. When the egg is mostly set, repeat the rolling process, then complete the omelette with the final one-third of the egg mixture.

9. Remove the omelette from the pan, then wrap in plastic wrap and chill until cold. Slice the omelette lengthways into four strips and use as a makizushi filling.

Negitoro
ネギトロ

Kanimayo
カニマヨ

Tamago
たまご

Seasonal delights

ONE OF THE BEST THINGS ABOUT konbinis are the local treats they put out during festivals and special occasions. Every Tuesday, 100 new items are released in Lawson stores, created by a development team located throughout Japan.

The country is divided into eight areas – Hokkaido, Tohoku, North Kanto, Metropolitan, Chubu, Kinki, Chugoku and Kyushu – each responsible for coming up with the next 限定 (limited-edition) item. And, for such a mighty task, only two staff develop the bread products nationally, with four to five overseeing desserts. For context, 200 new bakery and dessert items are released per year, made with local famous bread companies.

Limited-edition items are not a new thing in Japan, nor confined to the realms of konbinis. Almost every store you visit will have some sort of 限定 offering – perhaps a local specialty, or featuring a fruit that has just burst into season. (At the time of writing this book, it was Shine Muscat, which was featured in everything from parfaits to cakes to daifuku.)

In February, you'll find ehōmaki – giant lucky sushi rolls – designed to be eaten in a specific direction, silently, for luck that year. In March and April, as the cherry trees come into bloom, it's sakura mochi. In summer, you'll find premium roll cake for Roll Cake Day (6 June) and unagi kabayaki ju (grilled eel, believed to restore energy) on the midsummer Day of the Ox. In autumn, tsukimi keki – soft sponge cakes filled with a custard for Jugoya, the night of the harvest moon – are enjoyed, as are chūkaman (Chinese buns), served on the west coast of Japan with a lighter blend of shio (salt) and shoyu (soy), and on the east coast with a heavier soy-based sauce to cater to local tastes. In winter, there are the familiar bubbling vats of oden: the comfort food of fishcakes, tofu, konnyaku and egg, steeped in a dashi broth and served with a swipe of mustard.

As the year draws to an end, images of the prized items once reserved for department stores – strawberry short cake for Christmas, and osechi ryori, the traditional New Year's food served in jubako (a type of stacked bento box) – cover the banners and flags outside konbini stores. As always, these offerings are inclusive for the solo diner. From single tiers containing the lucky essentials of boiled prawn (shrimp), kuromame (sweet simmered black beans), red and white kamaboko (fishcakes), datemaki (sweet egg rolls) and kurikinton (sweet chestnut and sweet potato), to luxe multi-tiers for the ravenous, couples and families – brimming with abalone, ikura, Hokkaido roast beef and Hanasaki crab.

2 The hot snacks counter

ホットスナック

Chūkaman 46

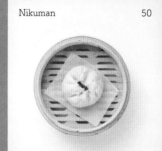

Nikuman 50

Pizzaman 52

Gomaanman 54

Fried chicken 70

Fried chicken bites 74

Karaage 76

Roast chicken 78

One of the allures of the konbini is the hot snacks section, filled with delicious, crispy fried morsels that call out for an after-work detour or to stave off hunger. This is where you will find the corn dogs – remnants of the konbinis' early days when they were modelled after Americana – and, since 1986, the juicy, succulent, addictive chicken nuggets that are Lawson's Karaage-Kun. Family Mart's Famichiki, a strong contender for the fierce best-fried-chicken battle among the konbinis, landed in 2006, while 7-Eleven's Nanachiki was introduced a decade later.

The hot snacks section is also where you'll find yakitori (grilled chicken skewers) glistening with tare (soy glaze), and in the autumn and winter months, soft, pillowy chūkaman (Chinese steamed buns). Our favourite season is winter, when simmering oden – fishcakes, tofu and konnyaku on skewers – appear in stores.

Potato & beef croquettes   61

Crab croquettes   62

Prawn croquettes   64

Ham & cheese croquettes   66

Rice buns with shigureni   80

Roll pizza   82

Chūkaman

中華まん

For the chūkaman dough

60 ml (¼ cup) warm water
6 g (¼ oz) dried yeast
60 g (2 oz) sugar
300 g (2 cups) flour (see note)
100 ml (3½ fl oz) milk
25 g (1 oz) pork lard
    (or vegetable shortening
    or oil), at room temperature

As autumn sets in, konbinis start putting up their banners for chūkaman (Chinese-style steamed buns) – also known as nikuman (meat buns), as their original fillings were traditionally steamed pork with onions or leek.

Once found in Chinatown districts such as Yokohama or Osaka's famed 551 Horai stores (where Osakans call them butaman – pork buns), they were eventually brought into the konbini fold, and – as with all things konbini – have since been stuffed with other fillings: pizzaman (page 52) filled with tomato sauce and melty cheese; special Hokkaido red bean paste and sesame seed buns (page 54); cheese curry buns; and even shrimp, mentaiko and cheese buns. Every konbini chain has their own filling, and just like the konbini hot-box chicken, each has their loyal fans. Below are our recipes for the three most popular ones.

1. In a small jug, mix together the water, yeast and one-quarter of the sugar. Leave for 15 minutes, or until foamy.

2. Sift the flour into a large bowl. Add the yeast mixture and remaining ingredients. Mix until a smooth dough forms, adding more water if the dough is too stiff, then cover and let rest for 1 hour, or until doubled in size.

Filling and steaming the buns

1. Knock the air out of the dough and divide into eight pieces. Shape each portion into a ball, then flatten with the palm of your hand into a disc.

2. Divide your chosen filling (see pages 50–55) into eight portions. Place one portion on each dough disc, then envelop the filling with the dough, pinching the dough closed.

3. Prepare a steamer basket (you may need more than one) by lining it with baking paper, and punching a few holes in the paper to let the steam through.

4. Place the buns in the steamer basket/s, leaving a 3 cm (1¼ inch) gap between each one and the walls of the basket, if possible, as the buns will expand. Let rest for another 15 minutes.

5. Prepare a pot (or two) with boiling water for the steamer basket/s to sit on, then steam the buns for 15 minutes.

6. Carefully take the steamer basket/s off the pot/s. Remove the buns from the basket/s and enjoy warm. The buns can also be chilled, then microwaved for 15–30 seconds to reheat.

Note

Asian grocers usually stock flour specifically made for steamed buns. If you can't find it, use plain (all-purpose) flour.

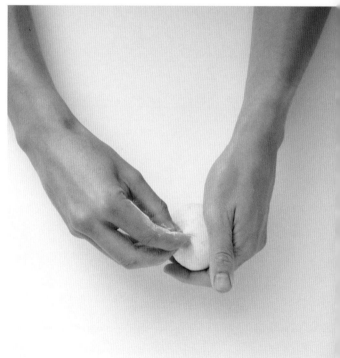

Nikuman

肉まん

1 quantity of chūkaman dough
(page 46), rolled into 8 balls

Filling

2 dried shiitake mushrooms,
    rehydrated in warm water
    until soft
50 g (1¾ oz) unsmoked bacon,
    finely chopped (optional)
½ onion, grated
2.5 cm (1 inch) knob of fresh
    ginger, peeled and grated
1 garlic clove, peeled and grated
250 g (9 oz) minced
    (ground) pork
1½ teaspoons lard
2 tablespoons soy sauce
1 tablespoon oyster sauce
1 tablespoon shaoxing rice wine
1 teaspoon sesame oil
1 teaspoon chicken stock
    powder (optional)
½ teaspoon salt
½ teaspoon ground white pepper

Here's a recipe for the traditional chūkaman pork filling.

The shiitake and onion add a deep savouriness to the pork, while the lard and bacon make the filling juicy and rich.

If you are feeling particularly Osakan, add a dash of hot English or Japanese mustard to your bun while eating it.

1. Drain the liquid from the shiitake mushrooms, then cut them into 5 mm (¼ inch) dice. Place in a bowl with the remaining filling ingredients, keeping them as cold as possible to prevent the lard melting. With gloved hands, mix together until the mixture is homogenous and the liquids have been absorbed into the pork mince.

2. Divide the mixture into eight portions, roll each portion into a ball, then fill and steam the buns as directed on page 46.

3. After steaming, the buns can be cooled and refrigerated for up to 2 days, then reheated for 10 minutes in a steamer, or in a microwave for 1–2 minutes.

Pizzaman

ピザまん

1 tablespoon olive oil
½ onion, diced
60 g (2 oz) bacon
   or ham, diced
1 garlic clove, grated
250 ml (1 cup) pizza sauce
1 quantity of chūkaman dough
   (page 46), rolled into 8 balls
300 g (2 cups) grated melting
   cheese, such as mozzarella
   or a pizza cheese blend

Another konbini case of East meets West, with the flavours of pizza encased in a soft, fluffy Chinese bun, tinted orange from the addition of ketchup to the dough.

When making the chūkaman dough on page 46, replace 50 ml (1¾ fl oz) of the milk with 60 g (¼ cup) ketchup and proceed as directed.

1. Heat the olive oil in a small saucepan over medium heat, then fry the onion and bacon for a few minutes, until the onion is soft. Add the garlic, turn the heat to low and continue cooking for 1 minute, until the garlic is cooked but not coloured.

2. Stir in the pizza sauce and simmer for 1 minute. Season with salt and pepper, then leave to cool.

3. Fill each dough ball with 2 tablespoons of cheese and 1 tablespoon of the sauce. Enclose the dough around the filling and pinch the edges together to seal. Turn over so the smooth side faces upwards. Rest and steam the buns as directed on page 46.

4. You will have extra sauce you can use for the ketchup rice and spaghetti napolitan on page 138, or the roll pizza on page 82.

Gomaanman

ごまあんまん

1 quantity of chūkaman
dough (page 46),
rolled into 8 balls
160 g (5½ oz) red bean paste,
either homemade (see below)
or store-bought
3 tablespoons black sesame
seed paste

While Chinese bao (known as 'man' in Japanese) are traditionally filled with either sweet red bean paste (anko) or black sesame seed paste (goma), the Japanese version combines the two favourites. The mild flavour and light texture of the bun balances the sweet and dense interior.

1. In a small bowl, mix together the red bean paste and black sesame paste using a spatula. If the mixture is too firm, add water, a tablespoon at a time, to loosen it.

2. Divide the paste into eight portions, roll into balls, then fill and steam the buns as directed on page 46.

To make your own sweet red bean paste

1. Place 200 g (7 oz) dried red beans (azuki) in a large saucepan, cover with water and bring to the boil. Once boiling, drain and rinse the beans. Clean the pan, return the beans back to the pan and refill with water. Boil, then drain again, and repeat one more time. After this third draining, fill the pan with fresh water, bring to the boil, then simmer for about 30 minutes, until the beans are soft. Drain the beans again, clean the pan, then return the beans back to the pan with 200 g (7 oz) sugar. Cook over medium heat for about 5 minutes, until the beans are well glazed in the sugar. At this point, you can mash the beans with a potato masher, if you'd like a smoother texture. Cool, then refrigerate until required; the paste will keep for up to 1 week.

からあげクン Cheese

国産チキン

ソースin からあげクン

たっぷりタルタルソース味

ソースin からあげクン
たっぷりタルタルソース味
KARAAGE-KUN Fried Chicken, Tartar Sauce
5個 | 税抜 **240** 円
254 kcal | (税込) **259** 円
卵・乳成分・小麦・大豆・鶏肉・豚肉・ゼラチン

この取っ手を引いてください

Lチキ　レッド
Fried Chicken, Hot
※唐辛子を使用しています
1個 | 税抜 **213** 円
255 kcal | (税込) **230** 円
卵・乳成分・小麦・大豆・鶏肉

Lチキ　レギュラー
Fried Chicken
1個 | 税抜 **204** 円
250 kcal | (税込) **220** 円
卵・乳成分・小麦・大豆・鶏肉

この取っ手を引いてください

Konbini today

'WE DELIVER TWICE AND SOMETIMES thrice a day to stores,' Mochimaru Ken-san of Lawson tells me. It's the reason behind the perfectly stocked and full shelves, even when groups of office workers swoop efficiently into the store just before their clock-on time starts, reaching for their tea, coffee and onigiri to start the day. We did a daily stakeout at two convenience stores within a busy city block in Tokyo over a week, and each time we re-entered, just after the morning exodus, the shelves looked untouched. Konbini staff truly possess a stealth mode that allows them to present a perfect universe – a constant restocking, primping and priming, so that the shelves are always full, the walls of o-cha and coffee neatly lined up, the onigiri and foil packaging perfectly plump.

The Japanese konbini is never sloppy or sub-par. With stores on every city block, and sometimes multiples in one, the competition is simply too fierce for slovenliness to be tolerated.

The karaage is always piping hot, freshly fried and juicy, lined up in little cardboard boxes ready to be whisked away and eaten. The cooked food is always fresh, an eagle eye kept on its expiration sticker. It's usual for all Japanese stores purveying edibles to bring your attention to the expiry times (if you're having something like a mochi or daifuku) or expiry days, to make sure you enjoy it in the window for which it was intended. Once, we picked up a humble bento from a konbini, and the cashier's eyes swiftly darted to the sticker on the package. 'Shou shou omachi kudasai' – 'Please wait a moment' – she apologised. The bento was near its expiration time; she stepped away to return with a fresh one.

In our shin ya (late night) wanderings, we have also ambled into konbinis where even though there were only a few sando, onigiri or bento remaining on the shelves before the stock was replenished early the next morning, they were always aesthetically presented, never lonely or forlorn.

Beyond the convenience of food and everyday products – and for travellers, the beacon of hope that is foreign currency via a 7-Eleven teller machine – konbinis offer a whole suite of services, much like a mini office. You can pay bills, sign up for umbrella hire, arrange Airbnb-type key pick-ups and smart phone rentals, and buy travel tickets and tickets to concerts and sporting events. Some have parcel lockers and parcel delivery, and 7-Eleven has coin laundry and bicycle-sharing services. In other konbinis, you'll even find Gachapon (miniature capsule toy) machines.

Some konbinis have a hybrid crossover with bookstores, and each is tailored to their local destination. Mochimaru-san shows us a picture of a Lawson in Fukushima near the sea. There's a section with all the fishing paraphernalia one might need – whether you've forgotten to pack an item of fishing tackle, need some refrigerated live bait, or you've made an impromptu visit to the ocean and decide you want to try your hand at fishing.

In areas further away from Tokyo, he tells us, konbinis sell fresh produce from local farmers or a collective of 17 'Lawson Farms' – each independently owned, but collaborating in a relationship that is mutually beneficial, as 'Japan-grown' is still a symbol of quality and preferred by the locals. In areas even more remote, tucked away in Japan's mountains where supermarkets and greengrocers are non-existent, Lawson konbinis, built into small trucks, bring the 'daily convenience' to townsfolk – including products on request.

We've been run over by salarymen at konbini in the mornings, and watched school-age children crouched outside the Gachapon machines after school, hoping for a cheerful thrill. We've seen high-school students in the manga aisle, trying to peek at the latest release or the thick, ever-enduring, *Shōnen Jump*. We've seen office workers lining up to warm bentos in the microwaves for lunch, and in the evenings picking up sozai (side dishes), or making snap decisions on beer/nihonshu/whisky and some 'drinking snacks' (dried squid, fish or jerky) to help them unwind.

We've seen office women pick out stationery and makeup, and while we've also seen some men take a peek or two at the gravure magazines not-so-discreetly tucked away in the magazine aisle, we've yet to see anyone buy the shirts, hosiery and undergarments you can also find. (Very handy if you arrive in Japan without your luggage, forget something on a short trip, or accidentally organise for your takkyubin luggage delivery to arrive one day later than you!) The konbini isn't just a convenience store, it's a one-stop shop for every part of Japanese life.

The hot snacks counter

The hot snacks counter

Korokke

コロッケ

This indispensable, creamy, deep-fried nugget is a Japanese must-have, found in butchers, shōtengai (old-style shopping strips) and fine-dining restaurants – and, for ease, the fried and freezer sections of konbinis.

Originally from France, croquettes were once filled with meat and later potatoes when they were brought to Japan in the 1800s. It was Einosuke Takaishi of Ginza's Shiseido Parlour who lent the current Japanese croquette its light, airy touch. Takaishi used béchamel in place of potatoes, creating a creamier croquette that has come to typify the Japanese korokke.

We have included several versions here. All use a panko breadcrumb, the secret to the extra-crispy exterior.

Single coating or double coating?

For solid or firm foods, such as tonkatsu (page 156), I recommend a single coating, as the item being deep-fried isn't going to fall apart. Also, if it's double-coated, the thickness of the coating may obscure the flavour of the main ingredient.

I recommend a double coating for softer foods, where the finished texture is helped by having an extra-crispy coating. For very soft fillings, a double coating also helps protect the centre from leaking out as it cooks.

Potato & beef croquettes

Makes 4

牛肉コロッケ

350 g (12½ oz) potatoes
1 tablespoon salt
neutral-flavoured oil, for frying
    and deep-frying
100 g (3½ oz) minced
    (ground) beef
½ onion, cut into
    1 cm (½ inch) dice
1 teaspoon sugar
1 tablespoon sake
1 tablespoon soy sauce

For crumbing
35 g (¼ cup) flour
1 egg, beaten
30 g (½ cup) dried or fresh
    panko breadcrumbs
shredded cabbage, to serve
mayonnaise, to serve

Across Japan, in old shopping districts, butchers have always sold beef croquettes to passers-by, to showcase the quality of their beef and lure new customers into their store. They're also a wonderful, warming snack for school students on their way home. Konbini tap into this nostalgia.

These croquettes are an inexpensive yet warm and filling morsel that can fill the space between meals, or be enjoyed as a meal on their own with rice and salad. They can also be made with left-over shigureni (beef with ginger; see page 80) in place of the beef, onion and seasonings listed here. Roughly chop the drained shigureni and mix it through the boiled potatoes, adding a little of the sauce to moisten and flavour.

1. Peel the potatoes, cut into 3 cm (1¼ inch) cubes and place in a large saucepan. Cover with cold water, add the salt and bring to the boil. Reduce the heat to a simmer and cook for about 15 minutes, until the tip of a knife goes through the potato easily.

2. Meanwhile, in a large frying pan, heat 2 tablespoons of oil. Fry the beef and onion over medium heat for about 5 minutes, until the onion is soft but not coloured. Add the sugar, sake and soy sauce and bring to the boil, then reduce the heat and simmer for 10 minutes to dissolve the sugar and allow everything to infuse. Taste and add more soy sauce, salt or sugar if required; the mixture should be very strongly flavoured, as the flavour will become milder after mixing with the potato.

3. When the potato is cooked, drain well and allow to stand for 5 minutes to steam off some excess moisture. Transfer to a bowl large enough to hold all the ingredients and mash lightly. You want a homogenous mixture, while still retaining large chunks of potato. Add the beef mixture and, using a spatula, fold it through the potato to thoroughly combine, without breaking up the potato too much. Season with salt and pepper.

4. Spread the mixture on a tray and allow to cool to room temperature.

5. Line a tray with baking paper. With gloved or slightly wet hands, divide the mixture into four pieces, shape into ovals and place on the lined tray. Do not stack them, as they will stick together. Cover and refrigerate for a few hours, or overnight, to firm up.

6. Set out three plates or shallow bowls to crumb the croquettes. Place the flour on one, the egg on the second, and the panko on the third. Line a tray with baking paper to hold the croquettes after you've crumbed them (they'll be sticky).

7. Crumb the croquettes by first coating them in the flour, then the beaten egg, followed by the panko, shaking off the excess after each coating. (At this point you can freeze the croquettes on a flat tray, then stack them in a container or a snap-lock bag and freeze for up to 1 month. Cook from frozen, adding an extra 2 minutes to the cooking time.)

8. Fill a large deep saucepan or deep-fryer with oil to a depth of 10 cm (4 inches) and heat to 180°C (350°F). Working in batches if needed to prevent overcrowding, cook the croquettes for 3 minutes, or until a skewer inserted into the centre comes out hot. Drain well and serve hot, with lots of shredded cabbage and mayonnaise.

Crab croquettes

カニコロッケ

90 g (3 oz) butter
90 g (3 oz) flour
300 ml (10 fl oz) milk
1 tablespoon olive oil
1 onion, finely diced
50 ml (1¾ fl oz) white wine
    or sake
100 g (3½ oz) cooked crabmeat
40 ml (1¼ fl oz) cream
1 egg, beaten
1 tablespoon chopped parsley
neutral-flavoured oil,
    for deep-frying

For crumbing
150 g (1 cup) flour
60 g (1 cup) dried
    panko breadcrumbs
2 eggs
1 tablespoon milk

The béchamel in these croquettes makes for a silky and luxurious filling. Once – and still – served at the finest French yōshoku restaurants in Japan, crab croquettes are now commonly found in konbinis. They are simple to make, and can be frozen so you always have some on hand.

These croquettes can be served on their own, or in a tomato sauce where the acidity balances the richness of the béchamel and crabmeat.

1. Melt the butter in a saucepan. Add the flour and stir over medium–low heat until the colour just starts to change. Add the milk in four batches, incorporating well after each addition. Set your béchamel sauce aside to cool.

2. In a separate pan, heat the olive oil, then fry the onion over medium heat for a few minutes, until soft but not coloured. Pour in the wine and cook until reduced to a syrup. Remove from the heat and cool to room temperature.

3. Line a tray with baking paper. Mix together the cooled béchamel sauce, crabmeat, cream, egg and parsley. Season to taste with salt and pepper. Form into eight ovals, then refrigerate on the lined tray for 1–2 hours to set the shape.

4. To crumb the croquettes, spread the flour on a plate, and the panko on another plate. In a wide shallow bowl, beat the eggs with the milk.

5. Crumb the croquettes by first coating them in the flour, then the beaten eggs, followed by the panko, shaking off the excess after each coat. Now dip the croquettes into the egg again, then the breadcrumbs, for a double coating. (At this point you can freeze the croquettes on a flat tray, then stack them in a container or a snap-lock bag and freeze for up to 1 month. Cook from frozen, adding an extra 2 minutes to the cooking time.)

6. Fill a large deep saucepan or deep-fryer with oil to a depth of 10 cm (4 inches) and heat to 180°C (350°F).

7. Working in batches if needed to prevent overcrowding, cook the croquettes for 3–5 minutes, until golden. Serve hot.

Prawn croquettes

海老コロッケ

2 tablespoons sake
1 teaspoon salt
300 g (10½ oz) raw
    prawns (shrimp),
    peeled and deveined
2 tablespoons mayonnaise
1 teaspoon potato starch
½ teaspoon white pepper
½ teaspoon chicken stock
    powder (optional)
2 tablespoons finely chopped
    leek, white part only
neutral-flavoured oil,
    for deep-frying

For crumbing

150 g (1 cup) flour
60 g (1 cup) fresh or dried
    panko breadcrumbs
2 eggs
1 tablespoon milk

The best ebi (prawn) croquettes are full of bouncy, sweet prawns and little else. The crisp panko coating exists to provide a crunchy contrast and holds the prawn mixture together. This croquette also works well in a burger bun, coppe pan (fluffy bun, page 210) or a rice bun (page 80), with shredded cabbage and mayonnaise.

1. In a bowl, combine the sake and salt, stirring to dissolve the salt. Add the prawns and massage until the sake turns cloudy. Drain the prawns and dry thoroughly with paper towel.

2. Blend half the prawns with the mayonnaise, and roughly chop the others. Mix together and add the potato starch, white pepper and the chicken stock powder (if using). Finally, fold the leek through. If the mixture is very soft, add some more potato starch to firm it up.

3. Form the mixture into four patties, place on a tray lined with baking paper and freeze for 1–2 hours, until firm.

4. When firm, crumb and fry the prawn mixture following the instructions on page 62.

Ham & cheese croquettes

ハムチーズコロッケ

300 g (10½ oz) potatoes,
    peeled and cut into 3 cm
    (1¼ inch) cubes
1 tablespoon salt
3 tablespoons flour
    or potato starch
1 egg, beaten
1 teaspoon curry powder,
    or a pinch of ground nutmeg
4 slices ham
4 slices cheese
neutral-flavoured oil,
    for deep-frying

For crumbing
35 g (¼ cup) flour
1 egg, beaten
30 g (½ cup) dried or fresh
    panko breadcrumbs
shredded cabbage, to serve
mayonnaise, to serve

Molten cheese and ham has always been a delicious pairing of ingredients, and given the Japanese love for curry and croquettes, combining the two was inevitable. The mashed potatoes spiked with curry powder give the croquettes an extra dimension, with the spice adding sophistication to the simple flavour of ham and cheese.

1. Place the potatoes in a large saucepan. Cover with cold water, add the salt and bring to the boil. Reduce the heat to a simmer and cook for about 15 minutes, until the tip of a knife goes through the potato easily.

2. Drain well and allow the potato to stand for 5 minutes to steam off some excess moisture. Transfer to a bowl and mash until mostly smooth. Add the flour, egg and curry powder and mix until combined. Season with salt and pepper to taste.

3. Divide the potato mixture into eight portions. Place one portion on a piece of plastic wrap, flatten to 5–7.5 cm (2–3 inches) in size, then layer a slice of ham and cheese on top. Cover with another potato portion. With the help of the plastic wrap, shape the croquette into an oval. Repeat with the remaining ingredients.

4. Freeze the croquettes on a tray lined with baking paper for 2 hours, or until firm.

5. Crumb and fry the croquettes following the instructions on page 61. If cooking from frozen, they'll take an extra 2 minutes to cook through.

この取っ手を引いてください

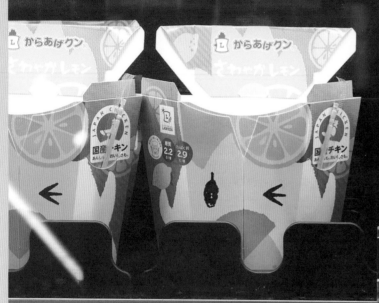

からあげクン
レッド
KARAAGE-KUN Fried Chicken, Hot
※唐辛子を使用して
います
5個
225 kcal
税抜 **220** 円
(税込 **238** 円)
卵・乳成分・小麦・大豆・鶏肉・豚肉

この取っ手を引いてください

The cult of Karaage-Kun: Karaage-Kun goes to space!

KARAAGE-KUN IS THE NAME of the cute chicken mascot for Lawson's karaage (fried chicken), and in testament to Japan's adoration for all things kawaii, has been around for about 40 years (its birthday is on 15 April).

Peer into the hot box on the counter of any Lawson store and you'll see a little army of Karaage-Kuns lined up, in flavours ranging from regular to Hokkaido cheese, lemon, red (the spicy version), tartare... and when we visited, a new, very muscular and tanned version called DeKaraage-Kun, with a garlic soy sauce flavour.

Part of the fun of visiting konbinis in different regions is that they often carry special lines with local ingredients (Tohoku had a limited-edition butter garlic Karaage-Kun with garlic from Aomori prefecture, for instance). Each of the main flavour Karaage-Kuns above comes with its own mascot. (Sadly, despite seeing them on the shelf in head office, we were informed they were not for sale, so we couldn't score a Karaage-Kun plushie.)

But back to the actual product. Even though we were in the middle of a heatwave in a meltingly hot early autumn in Tokyo, getting hot fried chicken made perfect sense... so we bought two packs – one DeKaraage-Kun and one cheese – because we were craving that burst of molten cheese hidden within the delicious nugget of salty, moist chicken. We've had karaage from dedicated karaage stores, and can attest you won't be getting a lesser product with a konbini karaage, particularly one from Lawson's range. They fry them frequently, but we don't know how they keep them so juicy, without a hint of sogginess.

Karaage-Kun is no ordinary chicken. On 8 June 2020, Japan's Aerospace Exploration Agency (JAXA) approved a special Space Karaage-Kun for their flight missions, after a three-year collaboration to develop 'meat in space'. This was to meet an expressed wish of Japan's astronauts: bite-sized versions of Karaage-Kun, freeze dried, with the flavour intact. (Of course, in head office, next to a JAXA certificate, there was an accompanying plushie for this, decked out in a mini JAXA uniform complete with space badges – also not for sale.)

It was no small feat. Space Karaage-Kun had to meet stringent requirements for long preservation and resistance to flight and microgravity stresses, enduring three years of testing before being given the all-clear.

Astronaut Noguchi Sōichi, on Expedition 64/65 aboard the International Space Station, was the first to enjoy Space Karaage-Kun – the humble chicken nugget that ventured where no other nugget had been.

Fried chicken

フライドチキン

4 boneless chicken thighs,
    skin on
neutral-flavoured oil,
    for deep-frying

Spice paste

1 small knob of fresh ginger,
    peeled and grated
1 garlic clove, grated
1 tablespoon soy sauce
1 tablespoon sake
1 teaspoon salt
½ teaspoon chicken
    stock powder
¼ teaspoon ground allspice
¼ teaspoon ground nutmeg

Wet coating

2 eggs
40 g (1½ oz) flour
1 teaspoon chicken stock powder
1 tablespoon soy sauce
1 tablespoon salt
½ teaspoon ground black pepper

Dry coating

100 g (⅔ cup) flour
100 g (3½ oz) potato starch

The stakes are high in the konbini fried chicken department, and every konbini chain has its loyal fans. There's camp Nanachiki, 7-Eleven's fried chicken; Lawson's Parichiki; and Family Mart's Famichiki – complete with packaging that boldly declares 'I am Chicken'.

Naturally, each has their secret recipe... Japanese karaage-style: soy-marinated with a light, crisp potato starch coating; or American fried chicken-style: marinated in a blend of spices with a thick, crisp, flour-based coating.

This recipe is for the American-style fried chicken. The flour-based coating encases a whole, boneless chicken thigh for a substantial snack or light meal.

1. Using just the tip of a sharp knife, poke small holes in the chicken thighs, through the meat and skin. (This will allow the marinade to penetrate all the way into the centre of the meat.) Place each chicken thigh between two sheets of plastic wrap. Using a heavy flat object, such as a meat mallet or frying pan, lightly beat the chicken, concentrating on the thicker sections, to make the thickness uniform.

2. In a bowl, mix together the spice paste ingredients. Add the chicken and mix very thoroughly so that every part of the chicken is coated. Cover the bowl and refrigerate overnight, or for at least 2 hours.

3. When you're ready to continue, line a tray with baking paper. Remove the chicken from the bowl and pat dry with paper towel to remove any excess water, but try not to rub off any of the spice mix.

4. Place the wet coating ingredients in a bowl and mix thoroughly. In a separate bowl, mix the dry coating ingredients.

5. One by one, submerge the chicken thighs into the wet coating, let the excess liquid run off, then coat in the dry coating, pressing the flour in so the entire chicken thigh is lightly and very evenly coated in flour, with no bare patches. Place on the lined tray.

6. Set an oven rack over a tray, ready to drain the fried chicken on. Fill a deep-sided frying pan with oil to a depth of 2 cm (¾ inch) and place over medium heat. Bring the oil to 160° C (320° F); it should bubble lightly when the end of a wooden chopstick is dipped into the oil.

7. Working in two batches, add the chicken to the oil; the chicken should bubble quickly, but not violently. Cook for 4 minutes on one side, then very carefully turn and cook on the other side for 4 minutes. (After 2 minutes, check the downward-facing side to ensure it's not becoming darker than golden brown; if it is, turn down the heat.) Remove and drain on your draining rack.

8. Turn the heat up under the frying pan to bring the oil to 180° C (350° F); the end of the chopstick should bubble more vigorously when dipped into the oil. In two batches, cook the chicken for 1 minute on each side, until the coating is crisp and uniformly golden.

9. Place on the draining rack for a few minutes, then sprinkle with salt and pepper and enjoy.

VARIATION

Spicy fried chicken
スパイシーフライドチキン

Mix 1 teaspoon ichimi togarashi or Korean chilli powder into the spice paste and another 1 teaspoon into the dry coating (depending on how spicy the chilli powder is, and how spicy you like it). Also add 1 tablespoon tobanjan spicy bean paste (also known as doubanjiang) to the wet coating. After frying, sprinkle with a little more chilli powder and a touch of chilli oil if desired.

If half your guests like their chicken spicy and the other half don't, simply add the spices to the dry and wet coatings after half the chicken has been coated in the plain versions.

Cheese
チーズ

After frying the chicken, sprinkle with about 50 g (½ cup) powdered parmesan or finely grated fresh parmesan.

Tartar sauce
タルタルソース

This sauce works well with all the fried foods in this book. Finely chop ½ onion and roughly chop 1 peeled, boiled egg. Place in a small bowl with 3 tablespoons chopped cornichons or pickles, 3 tablespoons mayonnaise, 1 teaspoon lemon juice and 1 teaspoon rice vinegar. Mix together, then season to taste with salt and pepper.

Fried chicken bites

チキンナゲット

100 g (3½ oz) tofu
400 g (14 oz) minced (ground)
    chicken, preferably from
    skinless thigh fillets
2 tablespoons potato starch
2 teaspoons chicken stock powder
2 teaspoons grated garlic
1 teaspoon salt
½ teaspoon white pepper
1 egg yolk (reserve the egg
    white for the coating below)
neutral-flavoured oil,
    for deep-frying

Coating
75 g (½ cup) cake flour
35 g (1¼ oz) potato starch
½ teaspoon baking powder
½ teaspoon chicken stock powder
½ teaspoon salt
½ teaspoon white pepper
1 egg white (saved from above)
250 ml (1 cup) water

Seasoning
1 tablespoon salt
1 teaspoon white pepper
1 teaspoon sugar

Note
The remaining batter can be
fried until crisp, then drained
and stored as tenkasu – a great
crunchy topping for udon or
soba noodle dishes, ochazuke
and okonomiyaki.

A twist on the famous Lawson Karaage-Kun, our fried chicken bites are in the style of chicken nuggets. Small but mighty, they pack a lot of flavour, and have a bouncy texture due to the addition of tofu in the mix. You'll need to start this recipe a day ahead, to drain the tofu overnight.

1. Place the tofu in a colander over a bowl, cover with paper towel and allow to drain overnight in the refrigerator to remove excess moisture.

2. The next day, mash the drained tofu in a bowl until paste-like. Add the chicken, potato starch, stock powder, garlic, salt, pepper and egg yolk. Using your hands or a spatula, combine until uniform and evenly mixed.

3. Fill a small bowl with water. Dip a teaspoon into the water, then take teaspoons of the chicken mixture and place them on a tray lined with baking paper. Repeat until all the chicken is used up, dipping the spoon in the water regularly to prevent the chicken sticking to the spoon.

4. Using damp hands, roll the chicken into uniform shapes, then briefly place the tray of chicken in the freezer.

5. In a bowl, whisk together the dry ingredients for the coating. Take the chicken out of the freezer and coat each piece in the flour mixture, shaking off and reserving any excess flour. Once all the chicken is coated, place back in the freezer, to stop them going soft while you're preparing the batter and the oil is heating.

6. Mix together the seasoning ingredients; if you have a spice grinder, you can blend them to a fine powder. Set aside.

7. Fill a large deep saucepan or deep-fryer with oil to a depth of 10 cm (4 inches) and heat to 160° C (320° F). Mix the dry coating ingredients with the egg white and water; the batter should be the consistency of thin cream.

8. Take the chicken out of the freezer. Working in 3–4 batches (depending on the size of your pan), coat the chicken in the batter and deep-fry for 1 minute, being sure not to overcrowd the pan. Stir gently to loosen any chicken stuck together, then turn to cook on all sides, cooking for 4 minutes in total. Transfer each batch to a wire rack to drain.

9. Turn the heat up until the oil reaches 180° C (350° F). Fry the chicken bites again in batches for 1–2 minutes, until golden brown. Remove from the oil, drain and toss with a few pinches of the seasoning.

10. Allow to cool for 2–3 minutes before serving. We recommend a side of mayonnaise mixed with a little sweet chilli sauce for dipping.

Karaage

唐揚げ

Serves 2

200 g (7 oz) boneless chicken
    thighs, skin off
neutral-flavoured oil,
    for deep-frying
150 g (5½ oz) potato starch
75 g (½ cup) flour
lemon wedges, to serve
mayonnaise, to serve

Marinade
2 tablespoons soy sauce
2 tablespoons sake
1½ teaspoons grated fresh ginger
1 teaspoon sugar
1 teaspoon salt
½ teaspoon roasted sesame oil

A simple dish of chicken marinated in soy and ginger with a light potato starch crust, karaage is the Japanese equivalent of fried chicken. It is sold not only in konbinis, but also at shōtengai (traditional shopping strips), izakayas and matsuri (Japanese festivals).

The thin potato starch coating lets the flavour of the chicken shine through. It is usually served piping hot, but is also great cold.

1. Combine the marinade ingredients in a bowl. Using just the tip of a sharp knife, poke small holes in the chicken thighs, through the meat. (This will allow the marinade to penetrate all the way into the centre of the meat.) Cut the chicken into bite-sized pieces, mix through the marinade, then cover and leave on the bench to marinate for 30–60 minutes.

2. Heat the oil in a deep saucepan or deep-fryer to 165°C (330°F).

3. Drain the chicken and dry well. In a clean bowl, mix together the potato starch and flour, and season with salt and pepper. Coat the chicken in the flour mixutre, shaking off the excess.

4. Add the chicken to the oil and fry for 2 minutes; you may need to cook the chicken in batches if your pan isn't big enough. Using a slotted spoon, remove the chicken from the oil and drain on paper towel.

5. Turn the heat up a little higher and bring the oil to 180°C (350°F). Deep-fry the chicken again for another 2 minutes, or until a skewer inserted into the chicken comes out hot.

6. Drain on a wire rack for 1 minute, then serve with lemon wedges and mayonnaise.

Roast chicken

2 chicken leg quarters
    (marylands), skin on
60 ml (¼ cup) sake
2 tablespoons mirin
2 tablespoons soy sauce
2 tablespoons sugar
1 teaspoon black pepper
1 garlic clove, grated
2 cm (¾ inch) knob of
    fresh ginger, peeled
    and thinly sliced

Roast chicken in Japan isn't a whole roasted bird as it is in the West, but rather chicken leg quarters – and while it doesn't quite top the fried chicken sales in konbini, it can still be found as a gentei (limited-edition) item around Christmas. Family Mart has an open-flame roasted chicken marinated in apples for sweetness, while Lawson spices theirs with black pepper and garlic.

Marinating the chicken overnight allows the flavour to penetrate the chicken and also makes preparation easier, as the leg quarters can simply be placed in a preheated oven when you're ready to cook it.

In our recipe we offer two versions: the black pepper and garlic one, and also a honey and yuzu version. The yuzu adds a fragrant citrus note to the caramelised honey. If you can't find yuzu, you can use lemon instead.

For honey yuzu roast chicken
Replace the pepper and garlic with 2 tablespoons honey and 1 tablespoon yuzu juice, and ½ teaspoon sansho pepper, if available.

1. Using a fork, prick the flesh side of the chicken pieces to allow the marinade to penetrate the meat.

2. In a large bowl, combine all the remaining ingredients. Place the chicken pieces in a large snap-lock bag. Pour the marinade in and seal, removing as much air as possible. Leave in the refrigerator overnight.

3. Preheat the oven to 200°C (400°F). Line a baking tray with baking paper. Remove the chicken from the bag and transfer to the prepared tray, skin side up, discarding the ginger. Pour the remaining marinade into a small saucepan.

4. Bring the marinade to a simmer and reduce by half, then take off the heat.

5. Meanwhile, bake the chicken for 30–40 minutes, brushing with the marinade every 10 minutes to achieve a rich, bronze colour.

6. When a skewer inserted into the thickest part of the chicken comes out hot, remove the chicken from the oven and brush once more with the marinade. Serve with a salad.

Rice buns with shigureni

ライスバーガー

Makes 2

300 g (10½ oz) warm
    cooked sushi rice
2 teaspoons potato starch
2 tablespoons neutral-flavoured oil

Shigureni (beef with ginger)

1 tablespoon neutral-flavoured oil
½ onion, thinly sliced
3 tablespoons sake
3 tablespoons mirin
2 tablespoons sugar
1 tablespoon tamari (see note)
1 tablespoon soy sauce
2 cm (¾ inch) knob of fresh
    ginger, peeled and julienned
250 g (9 oz) thinly sliced beef
    (from the frozen section of
    Asian grocery stores; look
    for a cut with even marbling)
handful of thinly sliced fresh or
    frozen burdock root (gobo;
    optional)

Suggested condiments

mayonnaise
lettuce
American cheese
tomato slices
pickles such as benishoga
    (pickled ginger)

The rice burger was first made famous by Japan's MOS Burger, which has wedged yakiniku (grilled beef), kakiage (tempura seafood and vegetables), unagi (eel), tsukune (meatballs) and even okonomiyaki between rice buns for years.

You can now find these in konbini in the freezer section. I prefer the crisp rice buns to regular buns, though they do fall apart more easily, so the burger is best eaten over a plate or wrapper.

The shigureni filling below (beef with ginger, poetically deriving from 'shigure', meaning 'autumn shower'), can also be served over hot rice, in onigiri or as the filling for the beef croquettes on page 61.

1. Start by making the shigureni. In a saucepan, heat the oil over medium heat. Add the onion and cook for a few minutes until soft, but not coloured. Add the sake, mirin, sugar, tamari and soy sauce and bring to a simmer. Add the ginger, then the beef. Cook for about 5 minutes, until the beef is no longer pink, then add the burdock root, if using. Cover with a cartouche (a round of baking paper with a small hole cut in the centre) and simmer over low heat for 10 minutes, or until the beef is tender and flavoured. Remove from the heat and reserve until required; the shigureni can be made a day in advance, then reheated.

2. Mix together the rice and potato starch using a spatula, being careful not to break up the rice too much. Divide into four portions and wrap each in plastic wrap. Working with one portion at a time, press each portion firmly into an 8.5 cm (3¼ inch) cutter, for a perfectly round rice bun, making it as flat as possible, and allow to cool.

3. Once cooled, heat the oil in a large frying pan over medium heat and cook the rice buns for 2–3 minutes on each side, until golden and crisp on both sides.

4. If using mayonnaise and lettuce, spread mayonnaise on the bottom rice bun, then add the lettuce to protect the bun from going soggy. Warm the shigureni in a saucepan. Using a slotted spoon, take the beef, letting the liquid fall back into the pan, and place the beef on the rice bun. Dress with your desired condiments and top with another rice bun to form a burger.

Note

If you don't have tamari, you can use soy sauce instead. The tamari does add extra umami to the beef, however.

Roll pizza

ロールピザ

120 ml (4 fl oz) warm water
7 g (2 teaspoons) dried yeast
¼ teaspoon sugar
¼ teaspoon salt
12 ml (⅓ fl oz) olive oil,
    plus extra for greasing
200 g (7 oz) tipo '00' flour

Topping suggestions

tomato sauce (2 tablespoons
    per pizza), chopped ham
    and cheese (¼ cup of each
    per pizza)
mentaiko, cheese and nori
corn, cheese and aonori
tomato, zucchini (courgette)
    and cheese
Torimeshi chicken (page 26)
    and cheese
Tuna mayo (page 26) and
    extra corn

Some of the best pizza shops can be found in Japan – the chefs trained in Italy before heading home to hone their craft. In konbini, this penchant for pizza takes shape as roll pizza – handheld hot pizza, designed for the solo diner, or to be had on the run.

Being Japanese, the pizza is a little different. The toppings can range from classic margherita or tomato, ham and cheese, to wild combinations like prawn (shrimp) mayo, mentaiko cream... or coffee with weiners (yes, sausages).

Make the pizza base and experiment using recipes throughout this book as toppings, to create your own signature pizza roll.

1. Mix the water, yeast and sugar in a large bowl. Allow the yeast to activate for 5 minutes. Add the salt, olive oil and flour. Knead by hand for 5–10 minutes, until a smooth ball forms. Place in a clean bowl, greased with a little olive oil, cover with a damp cloth and allow to rest for 1 hour, or until doubled in size.

2. Preheat the oven to 250°C (480°F), or as high as your oven will go. Place a pizza stone in the oven, if available, or use a baking tray or pizza tray.

3. Punch the dough down and divide in half. On a lightly floured surface, roll each dough portion out into a rough rectangle and cover with your favourite toppings. Fold the sides in by one-third to make a wrap. Bake for 10–15 minutes on the pizza stone or baking tray, until crisp.

4. Allow to cool for 2 minutes, then wrap the rolls in baking paper and enjoy immediately, or allow to cool and reheat later.

3 Osouzai

お惣菜

Black vinegar braised pork belly   86

Ebi chilli   88

Ume shiso chicken   90

Sanma kabayaki   92

Hashed beef   104

Kalbi-don   108

Kashmir curry   111

Keema curry   112

Potato salad   123

Blanched greens with miso sesame dressing   124

Kiriboshi daikon   124

Sweet vinegar pickles   126

Onion dressing   126

In an increasingly time-pressed society, osouzai – prepared foods – have become an indispensable part of everyday life. You'll find stores specialising solely in osouzai in depachika (the food sections of department stores), bustling with office workers picking up dinner before they head home.

Naturally, this phenomenon made its way into konbinis, where a generous amount of osouzai, both Japanese and yōshoku (Western-influenced), can now be found.

Here, we cover the comfort osouzai, from stews to sanma kabayaki (a classic of Pacific saury grilled with soy), hamburg steaks and different types of karē – the curries that the Japanese have adopted, made their own, and have a great fondness for.

Shōga-yaki 94

Hokkaido white stew 98

Hamburg steaks 100

Meatballs 102

Karē pan (Curry buns) 114

Pork vindaloo 116

Soy milk & pork nabe 118

Goya chanpuru 121

Black vinegar braised pork belly

Serves 4 as part of a shared meal

黒酢豚角煮

1 kg (2 lb 3 oz) boneless whole
    pork belly
4 tablespoons potato starch
2 tablespoons neutral-flavoured oil
50 ml (1¾ fl oz) sake
50 ml (1¾ fl oz) mirin
100 ml (3½ fl oz) apple cider
    vinegar or rice vinegar
1 litre (4 cups) dashi
    (page 245)
1 spring onion (scallion), trimmed
2 cm (¾ inch) knob of fresh
    ginger, peeled and thinly sliced
2 garlic cloves, sliced
120 g (4½ oz) sugar
100 ml (3½ fl oz) soy sauce
50 ml (1¾ fl oz) black vinegar
1 tablespoon oyster sauce
4 eggs

Braised dishes are most common in the osouzai section of konbinis as they keep their flavour when they are reheated. In fact, they often taste even better having had more time to marinate.

One of the most common osouzai is buta kakuni – braised pork belly – in which the tender, melt-in-the-mouth pork absorbs all the flavours of dashi, soy, ginger and garlic. The boiled eggs may be the best part, as they soak in the flavour of the cooking liquid while retaining soft yolks. This version adds a touch of vinegar to the sauce to add complexity and alleviate some of the richness, with the acidity bringing lightness to the dish.

1. Prepare the pork belly by cutting off the skin, leaving on as much fat as possible, then cutting the pork belly into eight pieces. Coat the pieces in 2 tablespoons of the potato starch, shaking off the excess.

2. In a large saucepan, heat the oil over medium heat. Sear the pork belly in batches, browning all sides evenly, taking care as the oil will splatter. Remove to a plate.

3. Drain the excess oil from the pan. Return the pork to the pan, along with the sake, mirin, apple cider vinegar, dashi, spring onion, ginger and garlic. Bring to the boil, then turn the heat down to a simmer. Cover with a cartouche (a round of baking paper with a small hole cut in the centre). Simmer for 40 minutes, skimming the broth regularly and adding more water if the liquid drops below the top of the pork.

4. Add the sugar, soy sauce, black vinegar and oyster sauce to the pan. Cover and continue to simmer for a further 40–50 minutes, skimming and topping up with more water if needed, until the pork is tender. Remove the pork to a plate to cool. Remove the garlic, ginger and spring onion from the sauce and allow the sauce to cool.

5. Bring a pot of water to the boil, carefully add the eggs, then boil for 7 minutes. Drain the eggs, then immerse in cold water and cool to room temperature. Peel the eggs and place in the cooled sauce, placing a sheet of paper towel on top to submerge the eggs. Cover both the sauce mixture and the braised pork and chill overnight.

6. The next day, remove the eggs from the sauce. Skim off and discard any fat on the sauce.

7. Pour 500 ml (2 cups) of the sauce into a saucepan (see note) and bring to the boil. Mix the remaining 2 tablespoons of potato starch with 3 tablespoons of water until smooth, then stir into the sauce until slightly thickened.

8. Add the pork to the sauce and simmer for about 10 minutes to warm through. Add the eggs, and simmer for another 3 minutes. Serve with rice and vegetables.

Note
The left-over sauce can be used in place of the dashi to make this recipe again, and will become more flavourful each time it's used.

Ebi chilli

海老チリ

2 tablespoons neutral-flavoured oil
2 garlic cloves, grated
1 cm (½ inch) knob of fresh
   ginger, peeled and
   finely grated
2 teaspoons tobanjan
3 spring onions (scallions),
   finely sliced, white and
   green parts separated
1 teaspoon sugar
½ teaspoon salt
½ teaspoon chicken
   stock powder
250 ml (1 cup) water
2 tablespoons ketchup
1 tablespoon potato starch
1 teaspoon rice vinegar
1 teaspoon chilli oil (optional)

For the prawns
250 g (9 oz) peeled and
   deveined prawns (shrimp;
   see note)
pinch of salt
potato starch, for coating

Ebi chilli has its origins in China's Sichuan cuisine – brought to Japan by Chef Chen Kenmin (Jianmin), father of Iron Chef Chen Kenichi.

Chef Kenmin altered the flavour of the dish to suit Japanese palates, serving it at his Sichuan restaurant Shisen Hanten, which opened in Tokyo in 1958. Ebi chilli would become Shisen Hanten's second-most renowned dish.

Crunchy, plump prawns (ebi) are coated in potato starch, then a slightly spicy sweet and sour sauce – one that is milder than its Sichuan origins.

Ebi chilli is best served with fried rice, or Chinese buns (mantou), as they do at Shisen Hanten.

1. First, prepare the prawns. Place the prawns in a bowl and sprinkle with a pinch each of salt and potato starch. Massage the prawns for a minute. Rinse and drain thoroughly, then pat dry. Coat the prawns in the potato starch, shaking off the extra starch.

2. Heat the oil in a frying pan over medium heat and fry the prawns for a minute on each side. Remove from the pan and set aside.

3. In the same pan, over medium heat, stir-fry the garlic, ginger and tobanjan until fragrant. Turn the heat down to medium–low and fry until the oil turns red. Add the spring onion whites, mix briefly, then add the sugar, salt and chicken stock powder, followed by the water. Bring to the boil, then stir the ketchup through.

4. Mix the potato starch with 2 tablespoons of water and add half to the boiling liquid, stirring to disperse and thicken. Bring back to the boil. If the sauce isn't thick enough, add the remaining potato starch slurry, otherwise discard.

5. Add the prawns back in, turn the heat to medium and gently mix. Leave to simmer for 1 minute, then stir in the rice vinegar and chilli oil, if using. Taste and adjust the seasoning with salt, sugar or vinegar to taste. Sprinkle over the spring onion greens.

6. Serve with vegetables and steamed white rice or fried rice.

Note
Buying peeled and deveined prawns takes a lot of preparation time out of the recipe.

Ume shiso chicken

梅しそささみ

2 chicken breasts
2 tablespoons potato starch
4 red or green shiso
    leaves (see note)
2 tablespoons ume
    (pickled plum) paste
4 mentaiko 'lobes', or 2 tablespoons
    mentaiko paste
2 tablespoons grated cheddar
2 tablespoons neutral-flavoured oil

This delicious dish has an addictive tanginess from the ume and savouriness from the chicken. While unusual, the combination of mentaiko (salted preserved fish roe) and cheese works, adding spiciness, complexity and richness.

Please add or subtract ingredients as you like. You can replace the mentaiko in each chicken breast with a few lightly cooked asparagus spears for more crunch, or add a sheet of nori inside for more umami.

This dish can also be panko-crumbed and deep-fried as for tonkatsu (page 156). Or, you can slice the chicken into thick rounds, thread onto skewers and grill in a pan or on a barbecue as yakitori.

1. Preheat the oven to 160°C (320°F). Line a baking tray with baking paper.

2. Cut the chicken breasts almost in half, leaving them all in one piece, to open them out like a book. Place the chicken between two sheets of plastic wrap and, using a rolling pin or meat mallet, gently flatten to a uniform 1 cm (½ inch) thickness. Season with salt and pepper and sprinkle with half the potato starch.

3. With the smooth side of the chicken facing down on the cutting board, place the shiso leaves in the centre, side by side, then spread the ume paste over the leaves. Place or spread the mentaiko over that, then a line of cheese.

4. Fold in the sides of the chicken, then roll up from the bottom. Season with salt and pepper and sprinkle with the remaining potato starch. Secure the seams together with toothpicks or wooden skewers.

5. Heat the oil in a large frying pan over medium heat. Place the chicken in the pan, seam side down, and cook for about 3 minutes, until browned. Turn the chicken over and cook on all sides until browned all over.

6. Transfer to the baking tray and bake for 20 minutes, or until a metal skewer inserted into the chicken comes out hot.

7. Remove the chicken from the oven and allow to rest for 5 minutes. Slice the rolled chicken and serve. This recipe can be prepared the day before, then chilled, sliced and added to bento (lunchboxes) the next day.

Note
You can use any soft herb, such as basil or parsley.

Sanma kabayaki

さんまの蒲焼

2 sanma (Pacific saury), either
    fresh, or thawed if frozen
2 tablespoons sake
2 tablespoons mirin
2 tablespoons soy sauce
1 tablespoon sugar
65 g (½ cup) peeled and grated
    daikon, squeezed
    of excess liquid

Sanma, or Pacific saury, is a delicious fish eaten in autumn, when they are at their fattest, sweetest and tastiest. They are normally grilled over an open fire with salt (shioyaki) when fresh. Sanma is so loved it can be found in konbinis in tins, or cooked kabayaki-style (grilled with a soy-based glaze), ready to pop back under the grill to warm through.

Sanma are usually sold whole, with the innards intact as they are edible and have a pleasant, mild bitterness. You can remove them before cooking if you prefer. Sanma can be found frozen in Asian grocery stores, but if you can't find it, any oily white fish, such as mackerel or eel, works well with this marinade.

1. Using a sharp knife, score the fish in the centre of the meat with an X on both sides, to help the fish cook more evenly.

2. Preheat the oven grill (broiler) to medium–high. Line a baking tray or grill tray with foil.

3. In a small saucepan, bring the sake and mirin to the boil. Leave to boil for 1 minute, being careful as the sake might catch fire. Remove from the heat and stir in the soy sauce and sugar until the sugar has dissolved. Set aside.

4. Place the fish on the lined baking tray. Place under the grill and cook for 6–8 minutes, until the skin blisters.

5. Turn the fish over, brush the soy mixture over the fish and continue grilling for a further 6–8 minutes, constantly watching to make sure the sauce doesn't burn.

6. Insert a skewer all the way through one of the fish and leave it there for 10 seconds. Remove the skewer and check the temperature – if the skewer is hot, the fish is cooked. If not, continue grilling, perhaps on a lower heat if the skin is starting to burn.

7. Transfer the fish to a serving dish. Eat the fish with the daikon to refresh the palate in between bites.

Shōga-yaki

生姜焼き

300 g (10½ oz) pork loin,
  cut into slices about
  5 mm (¼ inch) thick
  (see note)
2 tablespoons neutral-flavoured oil
½ onion, thinly sliced
2 tablespoons flour
  or potato starch
1 cup shredded cabbage
warm cooked rice, to serve

Sauce

2 tablespoons grated fresh ginger
2 tablespoons soy sauce
1 tablespoon sugar
1 tablespoon sake
1 teaspoon roasted sesame oil
few pinches of pepper

Translating as 'ginger grill' or 'ginger stir-fry', shōga-yaki is one of Japan's most cherished home-cooked dishes. It is said to have been invented by a tonkatsu restaurant in Ginza in the 1950s, and has since become a weeknight and bento staple.

It is most commonly served with shredded cabbage, rice and miso soup – and the gingery sauce also pairs well with different meats, mushrooms, tofu and vegetables.

1. Using a sharp knife, pierce the pork all over to tenderise it, focusing on the fat. Season with salt and pepper.

2. In a bowl, mix together the sauce ingredients and set aside.

3. Heat the oil in a large frying pan over medium heat. Add the onion and cook for about 5 minutes, until softened and slightly coloured. Push the onion to the side of the pan.

4. Coat the pork in the flour or potato starch, shaking off the excess, and sear in the same pan as the onion for 3–5 minutes. When nicely coloured, turn the pork slices over.

5. Pour in the sauce and allow to simmer for 1 minute, or until the pork is cooked.

6. Transfer the pork and onion to a plate, pour over the pan sauces and serve with the cabbage and rice.

Note

You can also use minute steaks or thinly sliced pork belly instead.

Konbini arenji

コンビニアレンジ

A popular way to cook for time-poor office workers and housewives is 'konbini arenji' – rearranging konbini food into a new dish. Konbini carry such a large variety of prepared food items (cooked chicken breast, onsen eggs, salads... and so on), that customers are expected and encouraged to mix and match to create something new.

A common trick is turning any onigiri (we recommend the shio salmon on page 25) into ochazuke by placing it in a bowl and adding hot dashi, or adding braised pork (such as the black vinegar pork on page 86) to instant ramen noodles in place of chashu (roasted pork).

Many of the dishes can be stuffed into a fluffy coppe pan (bun, page 210) to be enjoyed on the go, with fried chicken (pages 70–77) and potato salad (page 123) or coleslaw always a favourite.

Kushiyaki

串焼き

Kushi (skewer) and yaki (grill) are grilled or fried meats, found in yakitori-ya, kushiyaki joints and the hot boxes of konbinis – glistening with tare (sauce), or fluffy with panko. Skewered food in Japan can be broken into five main categories.

Yakitori

Grilled chicken (any part of the chicken, from the thigh to the wing, liver and organs)

Kushiyaki

Anything other than chicken, grilled

Kushikatsu

Panko-crumbed fried morsels

Kushi oden

Sticks of meat, seafood and vegetables braised in dashi

Other

Fruit skewers, karaage, hot dog skewers, and anything that doesn't fit into the above categories.

Here are a few ideas for skewers to serve at your next party.

Karaage

Skewer the fried chicken on pages 70–77 and serve drizzled with mayonnaise.

Hamburg steaks

Make the recipe as directed on page 100, but make the patties one-sixth of the size. Skewer while raw, then cook, skewered, in the pan with the sauce.

Negima

Using the torimeshi recipe on page 26, make the sauce in a small saucepan and reduce until sticky. Skewer the chicken, alternating with spring onion, then cook in an oiled frying pan or on a barbecue. When the chicken is almost done, brush with the sauce and cook until glazed.

Corn dogs

See page 176. Any normal hot dog (frankfurter, kransky) can also be skewered.

Hokkaido white stew

北海道クリームシチュー

500 g (1 lb 2 oz) boneless
    chicken thighs, skin off,
    or pork scotch
1 tablespoon flour
2 tablespoons butter
1 onion, diced
1 celery stalk, diced
1 carrot, peeled and diced
1 potato, peeled and diced
60 ml (¼ cup) white wine or sake
375 ml (1½ cups) fish stock,
    chicken stock or water
2 thyme sprigs, plus extra
    to serve
100 ml (3½ fl oz) cream
200 g (7 oz) raw scallops
white pepper
juice of 1 lemon

Roux
50 g (1¾ oz) butter
50 g (⅓ cup) flour

Hokkaido is famous for its seafood, meat, dairy and vegetables, and this comforting stew highlights the purity of those ingredients. To make a great version of this stew, simply use fresh, good-quality meat and seafood, and the flavours will come through clearly.

The key is to not cook the vegetables over too high heat. You want the ingredients to be cooked but not browned, as the finished sauce should be quite white. This stew is great with shichimi (七味 – Japanese chilli powder).

1. Coat the chicken or pork in a light dusting of flour. In a large saucepan, melt 1 tablespoon of the butter over medium heat. Working in batches if needed to avoid overcrowding the pan, fry the meat until browned on all sides. Remove from the pan and set aside.

2. Reheat the pan over medium heat. Add the remaining 1 tablespoon of butter, turn the heat down low, then slowly fry the onion, celery and carrot for 8–10 minutes, until softened, but not coloured.

3. Cut the browned meat into bite-sized pieces and add to the pan, along with the potato. Pour in the white wine or sake and stir to deglaze the pan. Add the stock and thyme. If the ingredients are not submerged, add more stock or water to cover.

4. Bring to the boil, skim off any scum that rises to the surface, then simmer for 10 minutes, or until the potato is cooked through. Add the cream and scallops and bring to a simmer. Season with salt and white pepper.

5. For the roux, add the butter to a microwave-safe bowl and microwave for 30 seconds to melt. Add the flour and mix well, microwave for 15 seconds, then stir. Repeat three times, for a total flour cooking time of 1 minute; the roux should be bubbling. While it's hot, mix in a little liquid from the stew, a tablespoon at a time, until the roux is a creamy consistency, then add it to the stew. Stir well.

6. Remove the thyme sprigs and finish with the lemon juice to taste. Transfer to a serving bowl, scatter with extra thyme sprigs and serve with rice.

Hamburg steaks

ハンバーグ

1 tablespoon butter
½ onion, diced
1 egg
25 ml (¾ fl oz) milk
30 g (½ cup) panko breadcrumbs
250 g (9 oz) minced (ground)
    beef or pork – or a
    combination of each
1 tablespoon ketchup
½ teaspoon ground nutmeg
½ teaspoon salt
½ teaspoon pepper
2 tablespoons neutral-
    flavoured oil

Sauce

50 ml (1¾ fl oz) red wine
200 ml (7 fl oz) demi-glaze
    (see note)
100 ml (3½ fl oz) ketchup
1 tablespoon oyster sauce
20 ml (¾ fl oz) cream

Note

If you cannot find demi-glaze,
boil 800 ml (27 fl oz) low-sodium
beef stock until reduced to one-
quarter of the original volume
and use this instead.

A favourite of young and old, hamburg steak is a dish that will never leave the konbini bento section. More than just a mid-week meal, it is also found in luxury restaurants, made with premium beef, and served with a rich demi-glaze sauce. The taste and texture is more akin to meatloaf than a hamburger patty, with a soft and juicy interior surrounded by a caramelised exterior – like the ends of a meatloaf.

This dish can take a little time to prepare, but once the patties are shaped, they can be frozen for weeks in an airtight container and defrosted for a quick meal. Serve with ketchup rice or spaghetti napolitan (page 138).

1. Melt the butter in a frying pan over medium–low heat. Add the onion and cook for about 10 minutes until softened, but not browned. Remove from the pan and allow to cool.

2. Crack the egg into a small bowl and whisk with the milk. Mix the panko through.

3. Mix the cooled onion through the minced meat, along with the panko mixture, ketchup, nutmeg, salt and pepper. Shape into two oval patties, slapping each piece in between your hands a few times to remove any air inside. Press an indent into the centre of each for even cooking.

4. Heat a frying pan with a lid over medium heat. Add the oil, then the patties. Place the lid on and cook for 3 minutes. Flip over, cover again and cook for a further 3 minutes, or until coloured on both sides. Remove to a plate.

5. In the same pan, make the sauce. Pour in the red wine and cook until reduced to a glaze. Stir in the demi-glaze, ketchup and oyster sauce and bring to a simmer. Place the patties back in the pan and simmer for 5–8 minutes, until a skewer inserted into them comes out hot. Turn off the heat.

6. Place the patties on serving plates. Add the cream to the sauce, mix to incorporate, then pour the sauce over the patties and serve.

VARIATION

Menchi katsu
メンチカツ

With these crumbed, deep-fried meat patties, the crisp exterior gives way to a juicy interior, as the crumbing holds in all the juices of the hamburg steak.

Shape the patties as directed above, but make them half the size, to give you four patties (two per person), making them easier and faster to deep-fry, without risk of burning. Instead of pan-frying the patties, coat them in flour seasoned with salt and pepper, then beaten egg, and finally panko breadcrumbs. Deep-fry at 160° C (320° F) for 6 minutes, until golden. Serve with either the sauce above, or tonkatsu sauce, ketchup, mayonnaise, mustard or simply lemon wedges. They are best accompanied by rice and shredded cabbage.

Meatballs

ミートボール

2 tablespoons neutral-flavoured oil

Meatballs

300 g (10½ oz) minced
   (ground) beef or pork –
   or a combination of each
½ onion, grated
50 g (1¾ oz) panko breadcrumbs
25 ml (¾ fl oz) milk
1 tablespoon mayonnaise
1 teaspoon chicken stock powder
½ teaspoon salt
½ teaspoon pepper

Sauce

1 garlic clove, grated
2 tablespoons sugar
2 tablespoons ketchup
2 tablespoons soy sauce
2 tablespoons rice vinegar

These meatballs are an easier, more shareable version of hamburg steak and are good as a side dish or as part of a larger meal. They are also commonly used as a kobachi – small bite – in a bento, paired with salad and/or rice or pasta.

Diced crunchy vegetables such as lotus root and water chestnuts are a favourite addition to these meatballs for texture, flavour and nutrients.

The punchy ketchup flavour of the sauce spiked with soy sauce and rice vinegar makes this a favourite for kids.

1. Combine all the meatball ingredients in a large bowl. Mix together using clean hands, massaging the minced meat to incorporate all the ingredients. Divide into 20 pieces and roll each piece into a ball.

2. Heat a large frying pan over medium heat and add the oil. Add the meatballs and cook, turning regularly, for about 10 minutes, until coloured on all sides.

3. Mix together the sauce ingredients, add to the pan and simmer over low heat for about 5 minutes, turning the meatballs in the sauce until they are glazed all over.

4. Transfer to a plate and serve, or refrigerate to add to a bento the next day.

Hashed beef

ハッシュドビーフ

200 g (7 oz) beef, thinly sliced
    (from the frozen section of
    Asian grocery stores; look for
    a cut with even marbling)
1 tablespoon flour
2 tablespoons olive oil
1 onion, sliced
½ carrot, peeled and cut into
    large chunks
150 g (5½ oz) mushrooms
    (one of or a combination
    of shiitake, button, shimeji
    and oyster)
2 garlic cloves, grated
1 tablespoon tomato paste
    (concentrated purée)
100 ml (3½ fl oz) red wine
400 g (14 oz) tin crushed
    tomatoes
125 ml (½ cup) beef demi-glaze
    (see note)
125 ml (½ cup) beef stock
2 tablespoons ketchup
1 tablespoon oyster sauce
1 tablespoon worcestershire sauce
1 bay leaf
80 g (½ cup) peas, fresh
    or frozen

To finish the sauce

3 tablespoons butter
2 tablespoons flour

To serve

2 cups warm cooked rice
1 tablespoon butter
4 teaspoons cream
1 tablespoon chopped parsley

Note

If you can't find beef demi-glaze,
boil 500 ml (2 cups) low-sodium
beef stock until reduced by half,
then use that in place of the
demi-glaze and beef stock.

Hayashi beef is part of Japanese yōshoku (Westernised) cuisine – a quick, French-influenced stew dating back to the Meiji era. It is distinguished by the use of thinly sliced beef, which greatly decreases the cooking time, and makes for a texture of sauce that goes perfectly with rice. Try this in place of a traditional beef stew. It's much faster, yet contains all the rich flavours associated with a long braise.

1. Coat the beef in the flour and a pinch each of salt and pepper. In a large saucepan, heat the oil over medium heat and brown the beef on all sides. Remove the beef to a bowl.

2. If needed, add a little more oil to the pan, then fry the onion and carrot for about 5 minutes, until soft. Add the mushrooms and garlic and continue frying until all the vegetables are cooked.

3. Add the tomato paste and cook for 1 minute, stirring constantly. Add the red wine and reduce by half, stirring constantly. Stir in the tomatoes, beef demi-glaze, stock, ketchup, oyster sauce and worcestershire sauce. Season generously with salt and pepper if required.

4. Add the beef to the sauce, along with the bay leaf and peas, and leave to simmer over low heat.

5. To finish the sauce, melt 2 tablespoons of the butter in a small saucepan. Add the flour and cook, stirring, until the mixture has a nutty aroma and is hazelnut brown. Add a ladleful of the stew sauce, stir to incorporate, then add another two ladlefuls. Mix well, then add this mixture to the simmering stew to thicken it.

6. Continue simmering the stew, stirring regularly so it doesn't stick to the base of the pan, for about 30 minutes in total, until the beef is tender. Turn off the heat and add the remaining butter.

7. Meanwhile, mix the warm cooked rice with the butter and season with salt.

8. Divide the rice between two plates, piling it to one side. Add the beef to the other side of each plate and top with the cream. Sprinkle with the parsley and serve.

Social infrastructure

'KAWAII!' IS THE FIRST THING that pops into my mind when we spy the
tiny bottles of shoyu, kewpie mayo and bulldog sauce on a konbini shelf,
all designed for the solo diner as part of seikatsu hitsuyohin, which translates
as 'daily necessities'.

Seikatsu hitsuyohin was further spurred a few years ago when the entire
world went into pandemic lockdowns, where dining out and being in close
proximity to other humans was deemed risky business. With locals frequenting
nearby konbinis for short runs rather than supermarkets and restaurants,
Lawson saw a need for daily necessities and leapt into it.

Konbinis had already been the place to find face masks (a part of Japanese
society long before the world adopted them), hosiery, shirts, undergarments,
false eyelashes, makeup and all sorts of 'daily emergency things you may need'.
During lockdown, however, in a collaboration with the retail company MUJI, the
range expanded to include all the essentials for a perfectly groomed individual;
we found MUJI pressure point massagers, MUJI nail varnishes in three classic
shades (clear, greige and red), bath salts, sheet and clay masks, and Imabari
towel handkerchiefs.

Japan's konbinis are classified by the government as shakai infura (social
infrastructure) – so much so that local governments are asking konbinis to
come into regional areas to fill an integral gap in Japanese society where there
aren't enough local residents to staff shops selling daily goods, supermarkets
and chemist stores. It requires only 2000 people in a 365-metre radius to
sustain a konbini, and in towns where more and more elderly folk are turning
in their driver's licence, nearby konbini stores are playing a more vital role
than ever – especially as the bento sold within meet nutritional values for
the obasan (grandmothers) and ojisan (grandfathers) who no longer wish to
or don't have the capacity to cook. Lawson even sends konbini trucks into
villages tucked away in the mountains, selling products to the townsfolk.

The role of konbinis as shakai infura became even more prominent after
the Tōhoku earthquake on 11 March 2011 (which Japan refers to as the
'3/11 earthquake'). The devastation it and the subsequent tsunami wrought
saw the closure of supermarkets in the affected areas. At this time of great
need, local konbini owners wanted to open their doors for their own community,
driven more by a noble intent to provide a service for society than thoughts of
economic gain. Lawson fully supported the konbini owners, air-freighting goods
into the region, with head office staff volunteering to drive to the area to assist
with supply. Lawson's ethos is, after all, one of 'Creating happiness and harmony
in our communities' – '私たちは'みんなと暮らすマチ'を幸せにします'.

Along with their deep-running tenet of omotenashi (gracious hospitality),
it is this passionate pursuit of community spirit that sets Japan's konbinis apart
from the rest of the world.

Kalbi-don

カルビ丼

400 g (14 oz) beef short ribs
(Korean-style, flanken cut),
separated
2 tablespoons neutral-flavoured oil
4 eggs
warm cooked rice, to serve
4 whole lettuce leaves
4 tablespoons kimchi
1 tablespoon roasted sesame seeds
2 spring onions (scallions),
thinly sliced

Marinade

50 g (1¾ oz) grated Asian pear
or daikon
2 cm (¾ inch) knob of fresh
ginger, peeled and
finely chopped
2 garlic cloves, finely chopped
1 spring onion (scallion),
finely sliced
2 tablespoons soy sauce
1 tablespoon sugar
1 tablespoon sake
1 tablespoon roasted sesame oil
1 teaspoon tobanjan

Korean dishes are becoming more popular in Japan, and konbinis are tapping into this trend. Kimchi, Korean pickles, Korean fried chicken, kimchi nabe (stew) bases and yukke (Korean beef tartare) are now found everywhere from the aisles to the freezer section.

Kalbi – Korean marinated beef short ribs – is one such dish, a great accompaniment to morioka reimen (page 144) or rice. The marinade is slightly spicy and sweet from the fruit and vegetables used, which also help to tenderise the beef.

Kalbi is most commonly seen in barbecued meat or yakiniku (焼き肉) restaurants where diners grill it themselves over a charcoal or gas grill. This recipe is made in a frying pan, but if you plan on having a barbecue, please try this marinade for that.

To eat, you can use the lettuce leaves as a wrap to encase a little meat, kimchi, rice and egg, or just mix everything together.

1. Put all the marinade ingredients in a blender and process until smooth.

2. Mix the marinade into the beef ribs, then cover and marinate in the refrigerator for 8 hours, or overnight.

3. When ready to cook, drain off the marinade and heat the oil in a large frying pan over medium heat. Crack the eggs in and fry, sunny side up, until cooked to your liking. Remove to a plate and keep warm.

4. Add the marinated ribs to the same pan in one layer and cook until browned, then turn over and brown the other side – about 4 minutes in total for boneless ribs, and 6–8 minutes for bone-in ribs.

5. Pile the rice into four serving bowls. Add the lettuce, then the ribs. Place a tablespoon of kimchi in each, then sprinkle with the sesame seeds and spring onion. Finally, top with the fried egg and serve.

Curry

カレー

By far the most popular food in the heat-and-eat section of konbini is curry. Even the smallest konbini will have a wall dedicated to curry in its various styles: Thai-style green and red curries, massaman curry, Japanese mild curries, curries with prawns (shrimp) instead of meat, and Indian-style curries in many forms.

Some parts of regional Japan have curry with local ingredients as their meibutsu (famous local goods), and top auberge (ryokans) often have curry made by their chefs as omiyage (souvenirs) in their gift shops. You can even find curry as a popular hiker's lunch in the Kamikochi National Park in the Japanese Alps — and curry packs are the perfect dish to heat up over a stove while camping, too.

The Japanese love curry so much, they created curry-filled buns — karē pan (カレーパン) — which are now so popular they have become a national dish.

On the following pages are a few of the favourite curries in Japan. Enjoy simply with white rice, or dress them up with naan, coriander (cilantro), pickled onion, and an onsen egg (page 244) or freshly cracked egg yolk. The egg makes the curry milder and more creamy.

We recommend basmati or long-grain rice to accompany these dishes.

Kashmir curry

カシミールカレー

155 g (1 cup) cashews
60 g (½ cup) raisins
4 tablespoons ghee or
   neutral-flavoured oil
3 onions, thinly sliced
1 carrot, peeled and diced
3 cm (1¼ inch) knob of fresh
   ginger, peeled and sliced
3 garlic cloves, grated
400 g (14 oz) tin
   crushed tomatoes
500 ml (2 cups) chicken stock
2 tablespoons soy sauce
1 teaspoon cardamom pods
1 star anise
1 bay leaf
1 shallot, thinly sliced, to serve
2 makrut lime leaves, shredded,
   to serve

For the chicken

600 g (1 lb 5 oz) boneless
   chicken thighs, skin off
½ teaspoon cayenne pepper
1 teaspoon garam masala
1 garlic clove, grated
2 cm (¾ inch) knob of fresh
   ginger, peeled and grated

Spice mix

2 tablespoons ground turmeric
2 tablespoons curry powder
1 teaspoon caraway seeds
1 teaspoon fennel seeds
1 teaspoon fenugreek seeds
1 teaspoon ground cloves
1 teaspoon ground coriander
1 teaspoon ground cumin
½ teaspoon ground cinnamon
½ teaspoon ground nutmeg
½ teaspoon cayenne
   pepper (optional)

'Karē' is a Japanese favourite with a rich history. First introduced to Japan in the 19th century by the British Empire and the officers of the Royal Navy, it has since become a staple – liberally poured over rice, udon, pasta and tonkatsu in households, humble restaurants and fancy yōshoku (Western-style establishments) alike. Among the milder, ubiquitous karē – flavoured sometimes with grated apples or honey – are darker, richer and spicier versions.

This one is a dark, sweet and sour curry from Kashmir for those who find the regular Japanese curry a little too mild. The sauce is fortified with blended cashews and raisins to round out the flavour of the curry, making it not too spicy, and adding a pleasant, viscous mouthfeel.

1. Start by preparing the chicken. Cut the chicken into bite-sized pieces and mix with the cayenne pepper, garam masala, garlic and ginger. Cover and marinate in the fridge for at least 1 hour, or overnight.

2. In separate bowls, soak the cashews and raisins in enough boiling water to cover. Set aside.

3. Mix together all the spice mix ingredients.

4. In a large saucepan, heat 2 tablespoons of the ghee over medium heat. Slowly sauté the onion for about 10 minutes, until golden brown. Add the carrot, ginger and garlic, then stir in the spice mix. Cook for a further 5–10 minutes, until all the ingredients have softened. Stir in the tomatoes and simmer for 10 minutes.

5. Transfer the mixture to a blender and purée until smooth, then pour into a large saucepan. Add the chicken stock, soy sauce, cardamom pods, star anise and bay leaf and bring to a simmer.

6. Meanwhile, rinse out the blender and blend the cashews with 60 ml (¼ cup) of water to a smooth paste, adding more water if necessary. Do the same with the raisins. Stir the cashew and raisin pastes into the simmering sauce.

7. Heat a frying pan over medium heat and add the remaining 2 tablespoons of ghee. Fry the chicken until brown on all sides.

8. Add the chicken to the sauce and simmer for 15 minutes, or until cooked through.

9. Season the curry with salt and divide among plates. Top with the shallot and makrut lime leaves, and serve with rice.

Keema curry

キーマカレー

3 tablespoons ghee
400 g (14 oz) minced
    (ground) beef
1 onion, diced
1 carrot, peeled and diced
1 tomato, peeled and diced
1 green capsicum (bell pepper),
    seeded and diced
1 garlic clove, grated
3 cm (1¼ inch) knob
    of fresh ginger, peeled
    and finely grated
1 tablespoon tomato paste
    (concentrated purée)
600 ml (20½ fl oz) chicken
    stock or water
1 bay leaf

Spice mix

2 tablespoons Japanese curry
    powder (or garam masala)
1 tablespoon cumin seeds
1 tablespoon ground coriander
1 tablespoon ground cumin
1 teaspoon ground cardamom
1 teaspoon ground cinnamon

To finish

2 tablespoons aka miso paste
1 tablespoon sesame oil
1 tablespoon honey
1 tablespoon soy sauce
4 onsen eggs (page 244)
coriander (cilantro) sprigs
    (optional)

Keema curry features minced meat, in this case beef, in a mild curry sauce. The curry is slightly sweet from the honey, with a Japanese flavour from the soy and miso. There are also plenty of vegetables cooked into the sauce, making it a healthy meal. It is one of Japan's most popular curries, and is also the filling for karē pan (curry buns, page 114).

The key to this dish is having the vegetables cut roughly the same size, so each mouthful is a balance of meat and vegetables.

Instead of making the spice mix below, you could use half a packet (about 100 g/3½ oz) of your favourite curry roux, adding it with the stock when the beef goes back in the pot for its final simmering. When using roux, taste before adding the miso paste and soy sauce. If it is salty enough, only add 1 tablespoon of miso paste and omit the soy sauce.

1. Place 1 tablespoon of the ghee in a large saucepan and heat over high heat. Add the beef and cook until browned, then remove from the pan and set aside.

2. Combine the spice mix ingredients in a bowl and set aside.

3. Place the pan back over the heat and add the remaining ghee. Cook the onion, carrot, tomato, capsicum, garlic and ginger until soft but not coloured. Add the spice mix and cook over medium–low heat for 8–10 minutes, until fragrant. Stir in the tomato paste and cook until it darkens.

4. Stir in a little water to deglaze the pan, then add the beef back in, along with the stock. Bring to the boil, add the bay leaf and simmer for about 10 minutes, or until slightly thickened.

5. When ready to serve, switch off the heat and stir the miso, sesame oil, honey and soy sauce through.

6. Serve over rice, topped with an onsen egg and a sprig of coriander, if desired.

Karē pan (Curry buns)

Makes 8

60 g (1 cup) panko breadcrumbs
neutral-flavoured oil,
    for deep-frying

Filling
300 g (10½ oz) Keema curry
    (page 112), cold
8 soft-boiled eggs (see note)

Dough
150 ml (5 fl oz) warm water
2 g (½ teaspoon) instant yeast
250 g (1⅔ cups) flour
2 teaspoons sugar
5 g (¼ oz) butter,
    at room temperature
½ teaspoon salt

These are one of our favourite Japanese buns, which you cannot
go past in a konbini or bakery.
    Curry buns are almost always coated in crunchy panko breadcrumbs,
providing an extra textural contrast to the creamy curry and egg.

1. To make the dough, combine the water and yeast in a bowl and leave for about 10 minutes, until frothy. Add the remaining dough ingredients and knead by hand, or using an electric mixer, until smooth and elastic. Place in a greased bowl, then cover and leave to rest in a warm place for 1–2 hours, until doubled in size.

2. Punch the dough down and divide into eight even balls, about the size of ice-cream scoops. With the palm of your hand, flatten the balls into 15 cm (6 inch) discs, place the curry in the centre (being cold, the curry will be firm) and press an egg into the centre of the curry. Stretch the dough to enclose the curry and egg and form into oblong ovals.

3. Place the panko crumbs in a large bowl. Lightly dampen the outside of the buns with water, then roll in the panko. Allow to rest for 30–40 minutes.

4. Fill a large deep saucepan or deep-fryer with oil to a depth of 10 cm (4 inches) and heat to 165°C (330°F). Place an oven rack on a baking tray for draining.

5. Working in batches, deep-fry the curry buns for 6–8 minutes, until golden brown, placing them on the rack to drain.

6. Eat immediately, or cool and refrigerate and enjoy cold. The buns can also be reheated in a 180°C (350°F) oven for 10 minutes.

Note
To soft-boil the eggs, bring a large pot of water to the boil, slide in the room-temperature eggs and cook at a high simmer for 7 minutes. Cool in iced water and peel.

Pork vindaloo

ポークビンダルーカレー

500 g (1 lb 2 oz) pork scotch
    fillet, diced
4 tablespoons ghee
1 bay leaf
1 cinnamon stick
2 tablespoons cardamom pods
2 dried red chillies, seeds
    removed
2 onions, diced
2 tomatoes, diced
1 tablespoon tomato paste
    (concentrated purée)
1 litre (4 cups) chicken
    stock or water
2 tablespoons soy sauce
200 g (7 oz) fresh lotus root,
    peeled and sliced
    1 cm (½ inch) thick
1 green chilli, thinly sliced

Marinade

30 g (1 oz) garlic, chopped
30 g (1 oz) fresh ginger,
    peeled and chopped
60 ml (¼ cup) coconut cream
1 tablespoon rice vinegar
1 teaspoon ground cumin
1 teaspoon garam masala
1 teaspoon salt

Spice powder

1 tablespoon ground coriander
2 teaspoons paprika
1 teaspoon cayenne pepper
1 teaspoon garam masala
½ teaspoon ground turmeric
½ teaspoon ground cumin
½ teaspoon black pepper

Vindaloo is commonly the most spicy curry in konbinis. Large chunks of meat (in this case pork) are simmered in an aromatic sauce with touches of chilli, coconut, garlic and ginger. Fresh tomatoes add acidity to balance the fieriness.

Soy sauce and lotus root are the Japanese touches, with the latter adding a pleasant crunchy texture and absorbing much of the flavour of the curry.

1. Combine the marinade ingredients in a blender and blitz to a paste. Transfer to a large bowl, toss the pork through until well coated, then cover and marinate in the fridge overnight.

2. In a large saucepan, melt the ghee over medium heat. Add the bay leaf, cinnamon stick, cardamom pods and dried chillies. Cook until fragrant, then add the onion and sauté for about 10 minutes, until golden and softened.

3. Add the tomato and tomato paste and cook until the liquid has evaporated. Stir in the spice powder ingredients and cook for 1–2 minutes, until fragrant.

4. Add the pork, along with the marinade, and cook for about 5 minutes, until coloured. Pour in the chicken stock and soy sauce. Add the lotus root, and a little more water if needed to cover the pork. Simmer for 30 minutes, or until the pork is tender; you can also let it simmer longer to reduce the liquid and make the flavour more intense. Taste and add salt if necessary.

5. Transfer to a serving bowl, top with the green chilli and serve with rice.

Soy milk & pork nabe

Serves 4

豆乳豚しゃぶ

10 lettuce or cabbage leaves
5 cm (2 inch) square of kombu
200 g (7 oz) pork belly, sliced
    about 5 mm (¼ inch) thick
1 large handful of thinly sliced
    vegetables, such as carrot,
    mushrooms, daikon
2 tablespoons sake
250 ml (1 cup) water
400 ml (14 fl oz) soy milk
2 tablespoons soy sauce
2 tablespoons sesame oil
2 tablespoons sugar
1 tablespoon grated garlic
1 tablespoon grated fresh ginger
1 tablespoon roasted sesame seeds
2 spring onions (scallions),
    thinly sliced
warm cooked rice, to serve

Sometimes sold as 'soy milk buta shabu' – despite the pork not being 'swished' around in the pot, which is where the name 'shabu' derives from – this is a very easy and comforting dish that's also healthy and filling. The soy milk adds a slight richness to the broth, and more vegetables can be added for texture, flavour and sweetness.

The simmered lettuce retains a satisfying crunch after cooking, offering a nice textural contrast to the other vegetables. The large craggy surface area of the lettuce also provides lots of places for the soup to cling to, so it might just be the most flavourful part of the dish.

1. Tear the lettuce or cabbage into pieces about the size of your palm.

2. Place the kombu in a lidded pot, then the lettuce or cabbage, alternating with the pork and other vegetables. Season with salt and pepper. Pour in the sake and water and bring to the boil.

3. Meanwhile, combine the soy milk, soy sauce, sesame oil, sugar, garlic and ginger in a bowl.

4. Evenly pour the soy milk mixture over the pork and vegetables. Bring back to a simmer, turn the heat to low, place the lid on and cook for 5 minutes.

5. Remove the lid and check the vegetables are tender and the pork is no longer pink. Remove from the heat.

6. Top with the sesame seeds and spring onion and serve with rice.

Goya chanpuru

ゴーヤチャンプルー

Serves 4

300 g (10½ oz) block of firm tofu
1 bitter melon, about 250 g (9 oz)
1 teaspoon salt
1 teaspoon sugar
1 tablespoon sesame oil
1 tablespoon neutral-flavoured
    oil, plus a little extra
200 g (7 oz) pork loin or belly,
    thinly sliced
2 eggs
2 tablespoons soy sauce
handful of katsuobushi (bonito
    flakes), plus extra to serve

Bitter melon can be a rather divisive vegetable. At first, the bitterness might be overpowering, but like coffee, once you've grown accustomed to it, it becomes addictive. Curing it with salt and sugar removes most of the harshness, leaving just a gentle bitterness.

This unique stir-fry from Okinawa is distinguished by its use of bitter melon, roughly broken tofu and katsuobushi seasoning, and its lack of sauce. Its simple nature belies its deep flavours, so please try it!

If you really don't like bitter melon, substitute it with other crunchy vegetables such as onion, capsicum or carrot – but please do try it with ゴーヤ (bitter melon) first.

1. Drain the tofu and sandwich between sheets of paper towel to remove the excess moisture. Leave for 1 hour.

2. Cut the bitter melon in half lengthways. Scrape out the seeds, then cut the melon into 5 mm (¼ inch) slices and mix with the salt and sugar. Massage gently to draw out the water, then leave for 10 minutes. Rinse under cold water and dry thoroughly.

3. Break the tofu into bite-sized pieces. Heat a frying pan over medium heat and add the oils. Cook the tofu, turning regularly, until browned, then remove from the pan. Cook the pork and melon separately in the same way.

4. Wipe out the pan, add a little more oil and gently cook the eggs until lightly scrambled. When the egg is almost set, return the tofu, pork and melon to the pan, along with the soy sauce and katsuobushi. Gently mix to reheat without breaking up the tofu. Taste and add salt, if desired.

5. Serve sprinkled with a little extra katsuobushi.

Yasai

野菜

Yasai is the Japanese word for vegetables, and below we cover some of the most popular ways in which these are prepared in Japan. From crunchy tsukemono (pickles) that accompany almost every meal to a delicious goma-ae (sesame) dressing and the irresistible potesara (potato salad), these are dishes to liven up any bento, lunch or dinner.

Potato salad

ポテトサラダ

500 g (1 lb 2 oz) potatoes
4 slices of ham, diced
100 g (½ cup) cooked
    corn kernels

Dressing

2 tablespoons mayonnaise
1 tablespoon neutral-flavoured oil
1 teaspoon dijon mustard
1 teaspoon rice vinegar
1 teaspoon sesame paste
1 teaspoon soy sauce

Pickled cucumber

½ short cucumber
1 tablespoon salt
250 ml (1 cup) amazu
    (page 126)

This izakaya staple of creamy potatoes with a slight kick of mustard and vinegar and crunch of pickled cucumber makes a crowd-pleasing side dish to any meal. It's also good in sandos (pages 185–193) or in a coppe pan (page 210).

What makes Japanese potato salad distinct from those of other countries is that the potato is broken – usually with a potato masher – rather than cut, so the potato texture is very irregular, with some large craggy chunks and some parts almost mash. Plenty of Japanese mayonnaise and pickles are essential for that izakaya flavour.

You can replace the potatoes with one-quarter of a shredded cabbage to make a delectable coleslaw. The pickled cucumber can also be replaced with any pickles you have on hand.

1. To pickle the cucumber, wash it well, then finely slice. Rub the slices with the salt and leave for 10 minutes to draw out the excess water. Squeeze the cucumber until mostly dry, then leave to soak in the amazu for at least 30 minutes, or up to 2 days.

2. Boil the potatoes in salted water until a knife pierces them easily. Drain and leave in the colander to cool and dry for 10 minutes.

3. Peel the potatoes, then place in a serving bowl. Mash lightly with a potato masher into irregular chunks.

4. Mix together the dressing ingredients and mix through the potato. If you prefer your potato chunky, be careful at this point not to break them up too much; if you prefer them smoother, break them up more. Allow to cool.

5. Drain the cucumber and mix through the potato with the ham and corn. Season to taste with salt and pepper and serve.

Blanched greens with miso sesame dressing

味噌胡麻和え

Serves 4

This complex yet simple salad dressing of creamy miso, sweet vinegar and sesame paste is wonderful with fresh greens or blanched, chilled vegetables.

500 ml (2 cups) Dashi (page 245)
bunch of leafy green vegetables, such as spinach

Dressing
1 tablespoon mirin
1 tablespoon sake
2 tablespoons shiro miso paste
1 tablespoon sugar
2 tablespoons sesame paste (white or black)
1 tablespoon rice vinegar
1 tablespoon roasted sesame seeds

1. Season the dashi to taste and chill. Prepare a bowl of iced water.

2. Bring a pot of salted water to the boil and blanch the greens, then chill immediately in iced water. Add to the dashi and allow to marinate for 1 hour.

3. To make the dressing, bring the mirin and sake to the boil in a small saucepan, then simmer for 30 seconds. Take off the heat and mix in the miso paste and sugar until smooth. Add the remaining ingredients and mix well.

4. Remove the vegetables from the dashi and serve with the dressing.

Kiriboshi daikon

切り干し大根

Serves 4 as a side dish

Kiriboshi daikon are sun-dried strings of daikon radish with a pleasant daikon flavour and mild crunchiness. If you can't find it in Asian grocery stores, you can use other root vegetables, such as regular daikon, kohlrabi or celeriac, cut into thin strips.

30 g (1 oz) packet of kiriboshi daikon, or 2 cups julienned root vegetables
1 tablespoon neutral-flavoured oil
½ carrot, peeled and julienned
2 fried tofu sheets (aburaage), sliced
200 ml (7 fl oz) water
2 tablespoons soy sauce
1½ tablespoons sugar
1½ tablespoons mirin
1 teaspoon dashi powder

1. If using kiriboshi daikon, place it in a bowl and add enough water to cover. Allow to rehydrate (following the packet instructions), then drain well.

2. Warm the oil in a frying pan over medium heat. Add the rehydrated kiriboshi daikon, or the fresh vegetables. Stir-fry to get rid of any excess moisture, then add the carrot and tofu and stir-fry for a further minute.

3. Stir in the remaining ingredients. Allow to simmer for 2–3 minutes, or until the vegetables have absorbed the flavour of the sauce. Season with salt to taste, then serve.

Onion dressing

玉ねぎドレッシング

Makes about 150 ml (5 fl oz)

With a little kick of spice and sweetness from the onion, this delicious, versatile dressing goes well with fresh garden greens. Bonito flakes add savouriness, while the rice vinegar and lemon juice round it all out with a gentle acidity.

½ onion, roughly chopped
½ garlic clove, peeled
pinch of katsuobushi (bonito flakes)
2 tablespoons soy sauce
2 tablespoons olive oil
1½ tablespoons mirin
1½ tablespoons sugar
1 tablespoon rice vinegar
1 tablespoon lemon juice
½ teaspoon salt

Put the onion, garlic and katsuobushi in a blender or food processor. Blend until mostly smooth, then add the remaining ingredients and some pepper. Taste and add more salt, pepper or vinegar as you like. Serve over a green salad.

Sweet vinegar pickles

野菜の甘酢漬

Makes about 1 cup

Pickles – or tsukemono – are a staple in Japanese culture, and one of the most common side dishes to go with konbini food. Their fresh, tangy crunch is a nice way to reset the palate, breaking up the richness of curries, the slick of fried food (age mono), the saltiness of ramen broths and the various side dishes in a bento. Almost any vegetable can be made into a pickle, the most common being cucumber, carrot and daikon.

Rubbing the vegetables with salt before pickling draws out some water, allowing more flavour to enter the vegetables.

1 cup peeled and thinly sliced vegetables, such as carrot, daikon and red onion, or smaller vegetables, such as baby cucumbers and mushrooms, washed and left whole
2 tablespoons salt

Amazu 甘酢
400 ml (14 fl oz) water
80 g (2¾ oz) sugar
55 g (2 oz) salt
120 ml (4 fl oz) rice vinegar

1. For the amazu (brine), bring the water to a simmer in a small saucepan. Turn off the heat and whisk in the sugar and salt. Stir in the vinegar, then chill in the fridge until cold.

2. Rub the vegetables with the salt and leave in a colander for 10 minutes. Squeeze the vegetables to release any excess water, pat dry with paper towel and cut into bite-sized pieces.

3. Add the vegetables to the cold amazu, ensuring everything is submerged. You might need to weigh the vegetables down with a small plate.

4. Leave overnight, then taste to see if it has a nice pickled flavour. If not, leave for another night. Serve with any of the savoury recipes in this book.

4 Bento:
More than rice

お弁当

Chicken over rice   134

Hiyashi chūka   136

Ketchup rice
& spaghetti napolitan   138

Lemon cream pasta   140

Sardine peperoncino   150

Seafood gratin   152

Tonkatsu   156

Katsudon   160

One of the characteristics of traditional Japanese cuisine are the many side dishes (okazu) that are served alongside the staple: rice. Back in the 18th century, in Edo Japan, bento were as simple as a single umeboshi (plum) with rice, carefully encased in bent-wood menpa boxes and used to sustain farmers, fishermen and other working-class people during the day.

For the noble classes, however, bento were lusher – luxurious okazu placed in lacquered or gold-leaf jubako (tiered boxes) or nobento (outdoor bento; essentially jubako with handles), and taken on hanami (cherry blossom viewing) or to kabuki (Japanese plays). Designed to be shared, these intricate bento were created with an eye for aesthetics and elegance – as they continue to be today. Even the humblest ekiben (train station bento) conceals a beautiful display of rice and okazu beneath its lid.

In this chapter, we provide easily transportable alternatives to the rice found in most bento. These dishes – which can be found in konbinis – can be enjoyed on their own, or paired with the osouzai in the previous chapter to create a bento.

Mentai okonomiyaki   142

Morioka reimen   144

Omu-yakisoba   146

Pasta with yamaimo & tarako   148

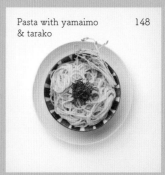

Katsu sando   160

Konbini greetings

A guide to the phrases used by konbini staff – occasionally spoken at lightning speed.

JAPANESE	ENGLISH	MEANING
Irasshaimase! いらっしゃいませ	Welcome!	A phrase you will hear not just in konbini, but in many establishments in Japan.
Shō shō omachi kudasai 少々お待ち下さい	Please wait a moment.	
Omatase itashimashita お待たせいたしました	Thank you for waiting.	
Otusgi no kata dōzo **Otsugi no okyakusama dōzo** **Otsugi de omachi no kyakusama dōzo** お次の方どうぞ・お次のお客様どうぞ・お次でお待ちのお客様どうぞ	The next customer waiting in line please	Kata 方 means 'person' and kyaku 客 means 'customer' (お o and 様 sama being formal honorific expressions). Kata and kyaku can be used interchangeably.
Kore hitotsu wo onegaishimasu これひとつをお願いします	Can I have one of these please?	This is useful for hot items on the counter which the serving staff member may have to take out for you. Kore これ means 'this' and hitotsu 一つ means 'one'.
Pointo kādo wa omochi desuka? ポイントカードはお持ちですか？	Do you have a point card?	A frequent question at most Japanese shops. To respond, you can say: **Motte imasen** 持っていません (I don't have it with me.) **Iie desu** いいえです (No.) **Daijoubu desu** 大丈夫です (It's okay – which in the Japanese context means no.)
Obentō atatamemasuka / Kochira atatamesuka? お弁当温めますか？・こちら温めますか？	Would you like your bento heated up?	This used to be a common question, but with most konbini having self-service areas with microwaves these days, you may not come across it. To respond, you can say: **Hai, onegaishimasu** はい、お願いします (Yes please.) **Kekkō desu** 結構です (It's fine – used as a polite decline.) **Daijoubu desu** 大丈夫です (It's okay.)
Nenrei kakunin botan wo oshite kudasai 年齢確認ボタンを押して下さい	Please press the button to confirm your age.	This is a standard question if you are purchasing alcoholic beverages. The cashier will usually gesture to the screen, where all you have to do is press the yes button to confirm that yes, you are indeed over 20.

Ohashi wo otsukeshimasuka? お箸をお付けしますか?	Would you like chopsticks?	With more konbini taking an environmentally friendly approach these days, you may have to ask for eating utensils. If they offer, you can use the responses of: **Hai, onegaishimasu** はい、お願いします (Yes please) **Kekkō desu** 結構です (It's fine – used as a polite decline) **Daijoubu desu** 大丈夫です (It's okay)
Sumimasen, ohashi ichi zen kudasai. すみません、お箸一膳下さい.	Can I please have a pair of chopsticks.	Hashi 箸 is 'chopsticks', ichi 一 is 'one' and zen 膳 is the specific counting word for chopsticks. For two chopsticks, use ni zen 二膳 For three chopsticks, use san zen 三膳
Sumimasen fo-oku / supun / sutoro-o kudasai. すみません、フォーク / スプーン / ストロー下さい?	Can I please have a folk/spoon/straw?	
Atatakaimono to tsumetaimono, fukuro wa betsu ni iitashimasuka? / Betsu betsu no fukuro ni oireshimashouka? 温かい物と冷たい物袋は別に致しますか?・別々の袋にお入れしましょうか?	Would you like your warm and cold items in different bags?	**Zenbu ishoude iidesu** 全部いしょうでいいです (You can put them together.) **Onaji fukuro de iidesu** 同じ袋でいいです (It's fine to put them in the same bag.)
Fukuro ni oireshimasu ka? / Fukuro irimasuka? 袋にお入れしますか? 袋いりますか?	Would you like these put in a bag? / Do you need a bag?	The cashiers are usually quick to pack the items away, but if you have a single or small item, you may hear this question. If you would like a bag, you can say: **Hai, onegaishimasu** はい、お願いします (Yes please.) **Fukuro wa irimasen** 袋はいりません (I don't need a bag.) **Kono mama de ii desu** このままで良いです (It's fine as it is.)
Shīru de yoroshii deshouka? シールでよろしでしょうか?	Can I put a sticker on this?	If you decline a bag, the cashier may ask you if they can put a sticker on the item to show it's been purchased.
~ en kara de yoroshii desuka? 〜円からでよろしですか?	I have received ~~~ yen from you, is that correct?	Most cashiers in Japan will confirm the amount they have received from you in cash verbally. A nod to this will do!
Reshīto wa yoroshii desuka? レシートはよろしですか?	Would you like your receipt?	In most cases, your receipt is handed to you with your change. These days, you can place your receipt in a small receipt collection tray on the register. If you don't see one, take the receipt with you. If asked, you can say: **Hai, onegaishimasu** はい、お願いします (Yes please.) **Daijoubu desu** 大丈夫です (It's okay.)

Useful Japanese counting words

While there are specific counting words for specific objects, these general ones cover most bases.

JAPANESE	ENGLISH
hitotsu ひとつ	one
futatsu ふたつ	two
mitsu みっつ	three
yotsu よっつ	four
itsutsu いつつ	five
mutsu むっつ	six
nanatsu ななつ	seven
yatsu やっつ	eight
kokonotsu ここのつ	nine
dou とう	ten

Useful Japanese konbini responses

JAPANESE	ENGLISH
Hai, onegaishimasu はい、おねがいします	Yes please.
Kekkō desu けっこうです	It's fine (polite).
Daijoubu desu だいじょうぶです	That's okay (declining.)

Chicken over rice

Serves 4

チキンオーバーライス

600 g (1 lb 5 oz) boneless,
    chicken thighs, skin off
2 tablespoons olive oil
4 tablespoons crispy fried
    shallots (optional)
¼ head of lettuce, washed, leaves
    separated, roughly chopped
2 tomatoes, cut into wedges
hot sauce, to serve (optional)

Marinade

150 g (5½ oz) Greek-style yoghurt
4 garlic cloves, grated
2 tablespoons lemon juice
3 tablespoons olive oil
1½ teaspoons oregano
1 teaspoon ground coriander
1 teaspoon paprika
1 teaspoon ground cumin

White sauce

80 g (2¾ oz) Greek-style yoghurt
40 g (1½ oz) mayonnaise
1 tablespoon chopped parsley
1 tablespoon lemon juice
1 tablespoon rice vinegar
1 teaspoon sugar
1 teaspoon salt
½ teaspoon pepper

Rice

300 g (1½ cups) basmati rice
    or long-grain rice
500 ml (2 cups) chicken stock
2 tablespoons butter, at room
    temperature
1 teaspoon ground turmeric
1 teaspoon ground cumin
1 teaspoon salt
1 teaspoon black pepper

Grilled chicken thighs marinated in Middle Eastern spices sit atop fragrant, turmeric-scented rice, all covered in a zingy white sauce of mayonnaise, yoghurt and lemon juice. This dish might not sound particularly Japanese – and it isn't. It's a dish from the Mr. Halal food truck that first set up shop in Marunouchi in Tokyo (and now Harajuku), and is based on a New York recipe.

When we visited Lawson's HQ in Osaki, Tokyo, we realised how competitive the konbini industry is, and how often they release new items and tap into trends. Konbinis have never shied away from taking foods from different cultures and adapting them to Japanese tastes. Many of the most popular konbini items have come from this embracing of foreign flavours, and the New York–inspired 'chicken over rice' is just one of them.

1. Trim any excess fat from the chicken thighs and check for any bones. Mix together the marinade ingredients and place in a snap-lock bag. Add the chicken, press out any excess air and seal. Massage the marinade into the chicken and place in the fridge for 2–4 hours, turning halfway through.

2. Mix together the white sauce ingredients and season with extra salt and pepper if needed. Refrigerate until required.

3. An hour before serving, prepare the rice. Wash the rice, mix with the remaining ingredients and cook in a rice cooker or on the stove, as per the packet instructions. Keep warm.

4. Remove the chicken from the marinade, discarding the marinade. Pat the chicken dry and season with salt and pepper.

5. Heat the olive oil in a large frying pan over medium heat. Pan-fry the chicken until golden brown, then flip over and cook until the second side is brown and the chicken is cooked through – about 12 minutes in total.

6. Take the pan off the heat, then cover and let the chicken rest for 5 minutes. Slice the chicken.

7. Spoon the rice into serving bowls and scatter over the fried shallots. On one side, pile the lettuce and tomatoes, and on the other side the chicken. Drizzle with the white sauce, and some hot sauce if desired.

Hiyashi chūka

冷やし中華

1 tomato
300 g (10½ oz) ramen noodles
2 slices of ham, shredded
½ short cucumber, seeded
    and shredded
½ carrot, peeled and shredded

Sauce

60 ml (¼ cup) rice vinegar
60 ml (¼ cup) soy sauce
3 tablespoons soy milk
    (or dashi, page 245)
3 tablespoons sugar
2 tablespoons sesame paste
2 tablespoons chilli oil (optional)
1 tablespoon roasted
    sesame seeds
½ teaspoon mustard
½ teaspoon dashi
    powder (optional)

Egg threads

2 eggs
2 teaspoons sugar
1 teaspoon sake
½ teaspoon salt
1 tablespoon neutral-flavoured oil

Perfect for summer, hiyashi chūka is a chilled noodle dish said to have been invented by a Chinese restaurant in Sendai, in the north-east of Japan, in 1937. It's distinguished by the colourful array of ingredients reaching upwards like Mt Fuji. Said ingredients can be humble, such as tomato, cucumber, carrot and lettuce, or luxurious by adding crab legs or prawns (shrimp). The idea is that the ingredients have the same shape as the noodles, so they can all be slurped up together.

Hiyashi chūka has a refreshingly salty and citrusy dressing that works beautifully with the springy ramen noodles. Effortless to make, it's one of the best ways to combat the hot and humid Japanese summers.

1. Whisk together all the sauce ingredients until the sugar has dissolved. Chill in the refrigerator until required.

2. Make the egg threads by whisking the eggs, sugar, sake and salt in a bowl until homogenous. Strain into a jug. Heat the oil in a non-stick frying pan over medium heat. When hot, pour in the egg, turn the heat to low and swirl the egg around to coat the bottom of the pan in a thin, even layer. Cook slowly, moving the pan around if needed to cook the egg evenly. When set, flip the egg over and cook for 3–5 seconds, until dry and not sticky on both sides. Slide onto a piece of baking paper and leave to cool. When cold, slice thinly and set aside.

3. Bring a small pot of water to the boil. Cut the stem out of the tomato and score the other end lightly. Place the tomato in the boiling water for 10 seconds, then transfer to a bowl of cold water. When the tomato is cool enough to touch, peel the skin off, then cut the tomato into quarters. Remove and discard the seeds, then thinly slice the tomato flesh.

4. Boil the ramen noodles as per the packet instructions, then rinse well in iced water until cold.

5. Pile the noodles into serving bowls and cover with the ham, tomato, cucumber, carrot and egg. Pour the sauce over and serve.

Ketchup rice
& spaghetti napolitan

Serves 2

ケチャップライスとナポリタン

2 tablespoons olive oil
½ onion, cut into 1 cm
  (½ inch) dice
½ capsicum (bell pepper),
  seeded and diced
4 button mushrooms, sliced
2 tablespoons diced ham
370 g (2 cups) cooled cooked
  rice, or 200 g (7 oz)
  spaghetti
60 g (¼ cup) ketchup
2 teaspoons soy sauce

Bento bases are usually plain white rice, chahan (fried rice), or something ketchup-based, like ketchup rice and spaghetti napolitan. Ketchup rice and spaghetti napolitan are two sides of the same coin: one made using rice and the other pasta. Both add a subtle tartness to bento, making them moreish and providing some vegetables. These dishes aren't confined to bento; you can make them as side dishes or main dishes in their own right.

For rice

1. Heat the olive oil in a large frying pan over medium heat. Stir-fry the onion, capsicum, mushroom and ham for about 5 minutes, until the onion is softened. Add the rice and stir-fry until warmed through.

2. Stir the ketchup and soy sauce through the rice and serve.

For spaghetti

1. Cook the spaghetti as per the packet instructions. Meanwhile, heat the oil in a large frying pan over medium heat and stir-fry the onion, capsicum, mushroom and ham for about 5 minutes, until the onion is softened. When the pasta is ready, drain it, then add to the frying pan.

2. Turn off the heat, mix the ketchup and soy sauce through and serve.

Lemon cream pasta

レモンクリームパスタ

2 asparagus spears
2 broccolini stalks
40 g (¼ cup) peas
1 lemon
200 g (7 oz) spaghetti
20 g (¾ oz) butter
1 garlic clove, grated
2 tablespoons white wine
150 ml (5 fl oz) cream
50 ml (1¾ fl oz) milk
2 thyme sprigs

A pasta that's just as delicious hot as it is cold, lemon cream pasta – adapted from Italy's pasta al limone – is a dish that speaks to Japan's love for creamy pastas. The citrusy lemon balances the richness of the cream, with brightness from the just-cooked vegetables. It might just become a weeknight staple!

1. Bring a large saucepan of salted water to the boil for the pasta and prepare a bowl of iced water.

2. Meanwhile, remove the woody ends of the asparagus and broccolini, then cut the greens into bite-sized pieces. Cut two slices from the lemon and reserve for serving, then zest and juice the rest.

3. When the water is boiling, drop in the asparagus, broccolini and peas and blanch for 1–2 minutes, until tender. Remove the vegetables and chill in the iced water. Drain and set aside.

4. Add the pasta to the pan of boiling water and cook as per the packet instructions.

5. Meanwhile, heat a large frying pan over medium heat. Add the butter and let it melt, then cook the garlic for a minute or two, until softened. Pour in the wine and simmer until reduced by half, then stir in the cream, milk and thyme sprigs. Season with salt and pepper.

6. Drain the pasta when done, reserving a little of the starchy cooking liquid, and add the pasta to the sauce. Stir until well coated, adding the reserved pasta cooking water as required to create a nice sauce. Stir the lemon zest and lemon juice through and remove from the heat.

7. Pile the pasta into two serving bowls and top each with a lemon slice.

Mentai okonomiyaki

Serves 2

明太お好み焼き

2 mentaiko 'lobes'
60 g (¼ cup) mayonnaise
1 tablespoon ketchup
80 g (2¾ oz) tempura flour
    or cake flour
80 ml (⅓ cup) water
75 g (1 cup) finely
    shredded cabbage
30 g (¼ cup) shredded cheese
50 g (1¾ oz) block of dry mochi,
    cut into 6 pieces
2 tablespoons neutral-flavoured oil
4 slices pork belly, 2–3 mm
    (⅛ inch) thick, or bacon
60 ml (¼ cup) okonomiyaki sauce
aonori, katsuobushi (bonito
    flakes) and benishoga
    (pickled ginger), to serve

Okonomiyaki, an Osaka staple, is a large savoury pancake normally made with cabbage and slices of pork, bound in a very light batter, topped with okonomiyaki sauce, mayonnaise, aonori (seaweed powder) and bonito flakes. Ingredients vary greatly from store to store and according to the customer's preferences. Okonomiyaki, after all, means 'what you like', grilled – so seafood and various vegetables often also feature.

This is a deluxe okonomiyaki, spiked with mentaiko (spicy cod roe), cheese and chewy mochi (rice cakes). Feel free to omit any of these ingredients if you don't like them or don't have them on hand.

For a softer texture, 60 g (2 oz) yamaimo (sticky grated yam) can also be added when mixing the batter.

1. Thickly slice one of the mentaiko lobes to mix into the okonomiyaki batter and set aside. For the other lobe, remove the roe from the sac, discarding the sac. Mix the roe with the mayonnaise and ketchup until you have a smooth paste. Place in a piping bag and cut a small hole in the tip.

2. In a bowl, mix the flour with the water to create a thin, lump-free batter. Add the cabbage and mix together well. Add the cheese, mochi and sliced mentaiko. Mix gently to combine, without breaking up the mochi and mentaiko slices.

3. Heat a lidded frying pan over medium heat. Add the oil, lay the strips of pork in the pan, then add the cabbage mixture. Press down gently and shape into a rough circle. Put the lid on and leave for 5 minutes.

4. Remove the lid, lift one side of the okonomiyaki and check underneath; it should be golden brown. If it's still pale, leave for another 3 minutes; if coloured, carefully flip over with two spatulas, as is done in Japan. Cover and cook for another 5 minutes. Once again, check the underside to see if it's coloured. If a skewer poked into the centre comes out clean, it's ready to be served.

5. Slide the okonomiyaki onto a serving plate, drizzle with the okonomiyaki sauce, then the mentaiko mayonnaise. Sprinkle with aonori and katsuobushi, and serve with pickled ginger on the side.

Morioka reimen

盛岡冷麺

150 g (5½ oz) cabbage kimchi
and/or radish kimchi, plus
2–3 tablespoons of the kimchi
pickling liquid
2 eggs
4 bundles of dried morioka
reimen noodles (or Korean
sweet potato noodles
or ramen noodles)

Broth

2 kg (4 lb 6 oz) oxtail,
cut into smaller pieces
1 kg (2 lb 3 oz) chicken bones,
cut into smaller pieces
1 beef shin, boneless, tied
into a roll
1 onion, halved
1 spring onion (scallion)
3 cm (1¼ inch) knob of
fresh ginger, sliced
2 tablespoons salt
2 tablespoons mirin
1½ tablespoons light soy sauce
1 tablespoon sugar
1 tablespoon gochujang

To serve

2 spring onions (scallions),
thinly sliced
½ Lebanese (short) cucumber,
thinly sliced
4–8 slices chashu pork or beef
4 slices watermelon or nashi

This cooling, almost salad-like, noodle dish from northern Japan is a popular lunch or dinner option in the summer months. Based on Korea's naengmyeon and brought to Japan by Yang Yongcheol, a Korean immigrant who wanted to recreate the flavour of his hometown, it is now one of the three great noodle dishes of Morioka – the other two being jajamen (a dish of Chinese origin), and wanko soba, soba served in many small bowls, one after another.

The idea of chewy sweet potato noodles in a cold beef broth served with fruit may seem strange at first, but once you taste it, you'll find it's perfectly balanced. The sweetness from the fruit goes well with the slight spiciness and sourness of the kimchi, and also the richness of the broth and meat. We recommend serving it with the kalbi from the kalbi-don recipe (page 108), as is done in Morioka.

In konbinis, you'll find the noodles packaged with the broth separately, so when it's time to eat and you pour the broth over, you get to enjoy chewy, not soggy, noodles.

1. Start by making the broth. Place the oxtail and chicken bones in a 10 litre (2½ gallon) stockpot and cover with water. Bring to the boil, then leave to boil for 5 minutes. Drain and rinse the bones. Place the chicken bones in the fridge.

2. Return the oxtail bones to the pot and cover with 8 litres (2 gallons) of fresh water. Bring to the boil, then reduce the heat and simmer for 2 hours, skimming regularly.

3. Return the chicken bones to the pot, along with the beef shin, onion, spring onion and ginger, and more water to cover all the ingredients, if needed. Return to the boil, skim off any scum, then reduce the heat and simmer for a further 3 hours. If you find the beef shin is sticking out of the water after skimming, cover the pot with a cartouche (a round of baking paper with a small hole cut in the centre).

4. Strain the broth, reserving the oxtail and beef shin, and discard the chicken bones and vegetables. When cool enough to handle, pick the meat from the bones, and cut the beef shin into 3–5 mm (¼ inch) thick slices. Discard the bones and sinew and keep the meat covered in the fridge until ready to serve.

5. Pour the broth into a container; you should have about 4 litres (4 quarts). Stir in the salt, mirin, soy sauce, sugar and gochujang. Taste and add more seasoning if desired. Chill until required.

6. When ready to serve, bring a large saucepan of water to the boil, and prepare a bowl of iced water.

7. Add the eggs to the boiling water and cook for 10 minutes. Remove with a slotted spoon and place in the iced water. Peel, then cut in half and set aside.

8. Add the noodles to the pan of boiling water and cook as per the packet instructions. Drain and immediately rinse in the bowl of iced water to stop them cooking further. Once cold, drain well.

9. Remove any fat on top of the chilled broth. Measure out 1.2 litres (41 fl oz) of the broth and mix with 2–3 tablespoons of the kimchi pickling liquid; it should taste a little sour and refreshing.

10. Divide the noodles among four bowls and ladle the cold broth over. Top with the beef shin and oxtail meat, and half a boiled egg. Add the kimchi, spring onion, cucumber, pork and fruit slices and serve.

Omu-yakisoba

オム焼きそば

200 g (7 oz) vacuum-packed
    or fresh ramen noodles
60 ml (¼ cup) neutral-flavoured oil
½ onion or 1 leek, white part
    only, thinly sliced
½ carrot, peeled and
    cut into matchsticks
75 g (2½ oz) cabbage,
    cut into bite-sized pieces
½ green capsicum (bell pepper),
    seeded and thinly sliced
2 garlic cloves, grated
40 g (1½ oz) ham, pork belly
    or bacon, cut into lardons
2 tablespoons okonomiyaki
    sauce, plus extra to serve
1 tablespoon oyster sauce
4 eggs, beaten
mayonnaise, for drizzling
1 tablespoon aonori
benishoga (pickled ginger),
    to serve

Omu-yakisoba is yakisoba (fried soba) in an omelette. The Japanese love eggs, and wrapping eggs around things is a good way of making dishes tastier, more filling, neater on the plate (or in the bento), and just a little bit fancier. Plus, there's that element of surprise when you cut it open to see what's within.

The yakisoba can be served without the omelette to make it simpler, or with a fried egg on top instead. The omelette can also be used to wrap fried rice, or the ketchup rice or spaghetti napolitan on page 138.

This dish comes together quickly, so have everything on hand, ready to go.

1. If using fresh ramen noodles, blanch them in a saucepan of boiling water for 1 minute, or until cooked, then drain and rinse in cold water. Drain again and coat in a little oil to prevent sticking.

2. Heat 2 tablespoons of the oil in a large, non-stick frying pan over medium–high heat. Stir-fry the onion and carrot for a few minutes, until slightly softened. Turn the heat to high, then add the cabbage, capsicum, garlic and ham. Stir-fry for another 3 minutes, or until the vegetables are cooked, being careful not to burn the garlic.

3. Add the noodles, stirring and separating them in the pan. If the noodles are stuck together very stubbornly, add a tablespoon of water to help loosen them. Season with pepper.

4. Pour in the okonomiyaki sauce and oyster sauce and mix until fully incorporated. Taste and add more okonomiyaki sauce if required, then remove from the pan and clean the pan.

5. Heat the remaining 2 tablespoons of oil in the pan over medium heat. When the oil is shimmering, add the beaten egg and swirl to coat the bottom of the pan. Turn the heat to low, moving the pan around to evenly cook the egg.

6. When the egg is almost cooked, add the yakisoba (noodle mixture) to the centre of the pan and fold the egg around it. Turn out onto a plate so the egg completely encloses the soba.

7. Drizzle with mayo and extra okonomiyaki sauce. Sprinkle with the aonori and serve with pickled ginger on the side.

Pasta with yamaimo & tarako

Serves 2

山芋と鱈子パスタ

200 g (7 oz) spaghetti
2 tarako 'lobes' (or mentaiko,
    if you like it spicy)
4 tablespoons grated yamaimo
    (see note)
20 g (¾ oz) butter
3 tablespoons mentsuyu
    (see page 25)
1 tablespoon mayonnaise
1 egg yolk
1 teaspoon instant dashi powder
2 tablespoons kizami nori
2 tablespoons shredded shiso leaf
2 tablespoons daikon sprouts
    or pea sprouts

This is a gentle-tasting pasta dish with a luxurious sauce made from yamaimo (mountain yam), which has a sticky and creamy texture. Outside of Japan, it can be difficult to buy fresh, but you can often find it in the frozen section of Asian grocery stores already grated. The texture can be challenging at first, but once you grow accustomed to it, you'll enjoy its unique mouthfeel. (Yamaimo is also great over soba dishes, both hot and cold.)

This dish also highlights tarako (pollock roe), but feel free to use mentaiko (chilli-spiced cod roe) if you prefer it spicy.

In konbinis, you can find this dish or a variation of it served cold. It's a great summer lunch and perfect for bento. Simply chill the pasta after adding it to the sauce, top with the remaining ingredients and pack.

Note

If yamaimo is unavailable, use 4 okra instead. Blanch the okra in a small pot of boiling water for 2 minutes, then drain and refresh in cold water. Cut off the tops, then finely chop and use in place of yamaimo.

1. Bring a large saucepan of salted water to the boil and cook the spaghetti as per the packet instructions.

2. Meanwhile, remove the tarako eggs from the sacs, discarding the sacs, and mix together in a large bowl with the yamaimo, butter, mentsuyu, mayonnaise, egg yolk and dashi powder.

3. Drain the spaghetti, reserving about 60 ml (¼ cup) of the cooking water, then mix the pasta and water into the tarako mixture to loosen the sauce and cook the egg yolk. Season to taste with salt and pepper.

4. Divide the pasta between two plates and top with the nori, shiso and sprouts.

Sardine peperoncino

いわしのペペロンチーノ

1 Japanese eggplant,
    about 120 g (4½ oz)
200 g (7 oz) spaghetti
100 g (3½ oz) tin of sardines in oil
2 dried chillies, or 1 teaspoon
    chilli flakes
1 bay leaf
2 garlic cloves, grated
small handful of cherry tomatoes,
    halved
2 tablespoons chopped parsley

As an island nation, Japan will add seafood to dishes other countries might add pork or beef to. This peperoncino is a good example. A simple garlic and chilli pasta is enhanced by the oily sardines to make a simple yet satisfying pasta dish. If you don't like sardines, use tinned tuna instead.

1. Cut the eggplant into bite-sized pieces. Place in a colander, sprinkle with a few pinches of salt and massage the salt into the eggplant – this helps to remove any bitterness. Set aside while preparing the rest of the dish.

2. Bring a large saucepan of salted water to the boil and cook the spaghetti as per the packet instructions.

3. Meanwhile, pour the oil from the tinned sardines into a large saucepan. Add the chillies, bay leaf and garlic. Place over medium heat and simmer for a few minutes, until the garlic turns soft. Add the eggplant and cook for about 5 minutes, until tender, then remove the eggplant from the pan.

4. Add the sardines to the pan, breaking them into large chunks with a wooden spoon. Season with a little salt and pepper.

5. When the pasta is cooked, drain, reserving 60 ml (¼ cup) of the cooking water. Add the pasta and cooking water to the pan and stir until the liquid becomes a sauce. Season with salt and pepper, add the eggplant and cherry tomatoes, then cook for a few minutes until warmed through.

6. Divide the pasta between two plates, sprinkle with parsley and serve.

Seafood gratin

Serves 4

salt, for soaking and rinsing
60 g (2 oz) raw prawns (shrimp),
  peeled and deveined
50 g (1¾ oz) raw scallops
100 g (3½ oz) white-fleshed fish,
  such as cod, skin off, cut into
  bite-sized pieces; you can
  also use salmon fillets
50 ml (1¾ fl oz) sake
200 g (7 oz) potatoes, peeled
  and cut into bite-sized pieces
100 g (3½ oz) short pasta such
  as macaroni, penne or fusilli
50 g (1¾ oz) spinach leaves
1 tablespoon butter
½ onion, diced
50 g (1¾ oz) button mushrooms,
  stalks removed, sliced
60 ml (¼ cup) white wine or sake

White sauce

50 g (1¾ oz) butter
50 g (⅓ cup) flour
400 ml (14 fl oz) milk
35 g (⅓ cup) grated parmesan
1 teaspoon chicken stock powder
½ teaspoon freshly grated nutmeg
white pepper
1 egg yolk

For topping

50 g (½ cup) grated parmesan
2 tablespoons panko breadcrumbs
1 tablespoon chopped parsley

In our first book, *Tokyo Local* (re-released with slight additions under the title *A Day in Tokyo*), we covered Japan's love for gratin and doria – a throwback to the height of Japan's yōshoku days, when French, Portuguese and Italian recipes were in vogue and later adapted to the Japanese palate.

Doria and gratin can still be found in grand hotels and yōshoku establishments around Japan today – and also in the freezer section of konbinis. We found a particularly luxe scallop gratin version in a fancy grocery store in Marunouchi.

Today, frozen prawns and scallops are often such high quality that the ones flown in from Japan are used in sushi restaurants. While we can't recommend you eat those from your local supermarket or Japanese grocery raw, they can be very delicious once cooked. Of course, if you live near the sea or have a good local fishmonger, you are fortunate!

This is a dish that can be made well ahead of time, then reheated for lunch or dinner. The other beauty of the gratin is how flexible it is. You can focus on your favourite seafood, or use chicken instead – and the pasta can be swapped with a layer of cooked rice, mixed with a little butter in the bottom of the baking dish, to turn it into a doria.

1. In a large bowl, dissolve 3 tablespoons of salt in 500 ml (2 cups) of water. Add the prawns, scallops and fish, then wash them in the salty liquid for about 30 seconds. Drain. Mix the sake with 1 teaspoon of salt, add the seafood and gently massage; the sake should go cloudy. Drain the seafood, then pat dry. Cut the prawns and scallops into bite-sized pieces and set aside.

2. To make the white sauce, add the butter and flour to a saucepan and cook over medium heat, stirring often, for a few minutes, until you get a nutty aroma and blond colour. Add the milk in four batches, mixing well each time until smooth. Bring to a simmer, then remove from the heat. Add the cheese, stock powder, nutmeg, salt and white pepper to taste, and, finally, the egg yolk. Mix thoroughly and set aside.

3. Butter a large baking dish.

4. Place a large pot of cold water over medium heat. Add the potato and a few pinches of salt. Bring to the boil, then simmer for 15 minutes, or until a knife goes through the centre of the potato with just a little resistance. Using a slotted spoon, remove the potato from the water and set aside.

5. Blanch the pasta in the same pot of boiling water, cooking for 1 minute less than the packet instructions suggest. Scoop the pasta out of the pan, into a colander, and set aside to drain.

6. Now blanch the spinach in the boiling water for 30 seconds. Drain, rinse under cold water and squeeze out the excess liquid. Roughly chop, then add to the pasta.

7. In a large saucepan, melt the butter and cook the onion over low heat for about 5 minutes, until softened. Turn the heat to medium. Working in batches if needed to prevent overcrowding, cook the seafood and mushroom until the seafood is almost done.

8. Add the wine and cook until almost completely evaporated, then add the pasta, spinach, potato and white sauce. Stirring constantly, cook over low heat until the sauce has thickened. Taste and season with salt and white pepper if needed.

9. Transfer the seafood mixture to the buttered baking dish, then sprinkle with the cheese and panko. At this point, you can chill the gratin in the refrigerator and cook at a later time. If serving now, cook under the oven grill (broiler) until the cheese has melted and the top is brown. To cook from cold, bake at 180° C (350° F) for 30 minutes, or until hot in the centre.

10. Sprinkle with the parsley and serve.

Tonkatsu

とんかつ

2 boneless pork loin fillets,
    each 2 cm (¾ inch) thick
75 g (½ cup) flour
½ teaspoon salt
½ teaspoon pepper
1 egg, beaten
60 g (1 cup) panko breadcrumbs
neutral-flavoured oil, for
    deep-frying

Brine

1 litre (4 cups) water
3 tablespoons salt
80 g (⅓ cup) sugar
1 tablespoon whole black
    peppercorns

One of Japan's favourite foods (and particularly great with beer), at its simplest, tonkatsu is a piece of pork, usually sirloin or tenderloin, breaded in panko breadcrumbs and deep-fried. These delicious hot morsels can be found in depachika, butchers and in specialty restaurants, with their own tonkatsu sauce mix or using special pork breeds such as Kurobuta or Kinkaton.

Although most konbini tonkatsu lose the crispness in their coating, the pork is still very moist, with the panko acting as a sponge to catch all the tonkatsu sauce – a sweet and sour sauce made from slow-simmered fruits and vegetables. Konbini tonkatsu remind us of the regions in Japan that serve their tonkatsu covered in tonkatsu sauce. These are just as delicious as the versions with the sauce on the side.

Japan's love for tonkatsu and its versatility means you'll find it in many forms – appearing in sandwiches, bentos and rice bowls (donburi). On the next few pages you'll find some popular preparations.

1. In a saucepan, combine the brine ingredients. Heat, stirring until the salt and sugar have dissolved, then remove from the heat and allow to cool.

2. Remove the skin from the pork and trim away the excess fat; score any remaining fat with a sharp knife. Add the pork to the cooled brine and refrigerate for 2 hours.

3. Remove the pork from the brine, discard the brine and pat the pork dry.

4. On a plate or shallow bowl, mix the flour with the salt and pepper. Crumb the pork by first coating in the seasoned flour, then the beaten egg and finally the panko, pressing the breadcrumbs into the pork well to fully coat it.

5. Fill a large deep saucepan or deep-fryer with oil to a depth of 10 cm (4 inches) and heat to 170° C (340° F). Gently slide the pork in and cook for 4 minutes, turning halfway through. Remove the pork from the oil; if a cake skewer inserted into the pork comes out hot, the pork is done. Place on a wire rack set over a baking tray and allow to rest and drain the excess oil for 2 minutes.

6. Slice the pork and serve with rice, shredded cabbage and a sauce of your choice (see opposite), or simply wedges of lemon.

Tonkatsu sauce

とんかつソース

Serves 2

A simple tonkatsu sauce for when you can't find it in stores. You can also adjust the amount of mustard, or use a different mustard to make it more spicy.

3 tablespoons oyster sauce
2 tablespoons ketchup
2 tablespoons roasted sesame seeds
1 tablespoon soy sauce
1 tablespoon mayonnaise
1 tablespoon sake
1 teaspoon sugar
1 tablespoon dijon mustard

Mix all the ingredients together and serve with tonkatsu.

Negi shio

ネギ塩

Serves 2, with some left over

We first tasted this at a very good tonkatsu restaurant in Shibuya. Fresh and spicy from the garlic and onion, this easy alternative to tonkatsu sauce is also a great accompaniment to other fried foods.

120 g (1 cup) very finely chopped spring onion (scallion), white part only
2 garlic cloves, finely grated
2 tablespoons sake
1 tablespoon salt

Mix all the ingredients together, then serve with tonkatsu, with some lemon wedges on the side.

Miso katsu

味噌カツ

Serves 2

A Nagoya specialty of dark, aged hatcho miso sauce that is their substitute for tonkatsu sauce.

2 tablespoons sake
1 tablespoon mirin
1–2 tablespoons Dashi (page 245) or water, to loosen
1 tablespoon hatcho miso paste
1 tablespoon roasted sesame seeds
1 tablespoon sugar

In a small saucepan, heat the sake and mirin until boiling. Allow to boil for 30 seconds, then take off the heat. Whisk in the remaining ingredients, adding more dashi to loosen if the sauce is very thick. Serve, poured over tonkatsu.

Katsudon

カツ丼

Serves 1

A comforting dish where the panko coating of the tonkatsu turns soft, having soaked up the flavour of the dashi and onions. This is very quick to make if you have store-bought or left-over tonkatsu.

neutral-flavoured oil, for pan-frying
¼ onion, thinly sliced
60 ml (¼ cup) Dashi (page 245)
1 teaspoon sugar
1 tablespoon soy sauce
1 tablespoon mirin
2 eggs
1 cooked tonkatsu (page 156), sliced
warm cooked rice, to serve
1 spring onion (scallion), thinly sliced

1. In a small frying pan, heat a little oil, then cook the onion over medium heat for about 3 minutes, until softened. Add the dashi, sugar, soy sauce and mirin and bring to the boil.

2. Whisk the eggs in a bowl. Place the tonkatsu in the frying pan, then pour the whisked egg over. Turn the heat to low, place a lid on and cook for about 2 minutes, until the tonkatsu is heated through and the egg is set.

3. Slide the tonkatsu and egg atop a bowl of hot rice. Serve drizzled with any pan juices and garnished with the spring onion.

Katsu sando

カツサンド

Serves 1

1. Cut off two thick slices of fresh shokupan (page 184). Coat each slice of bread corner to corner with a layer of tonkatsu sauce (made without sesame seeds; see page 158). Add a layer of cabbage to one piece, if you like, then place a cooked tonkatsu (page 156) on top and sandwich together. Wrap tightly in baking paper, foil or plastic wrap. Press gently between two porcelain or ceramic plates for 5 minutes.

2. With the sandwich still wrapped, cut off the bread crusts, and cut the sando in half. Remove the wrapping and serve.

From the Konbini shelves

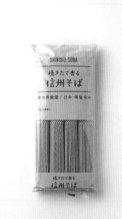

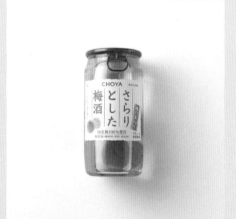

Bento: More than rice

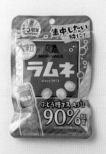

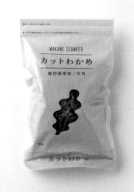

5 Bakery

ベーカリー

Hotcake mix 166

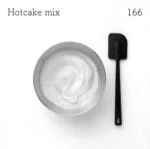

Hotcakes 168

Mochi donuts 170

Old-fashioned donuts 172

Pound cake 174

Corn dog 176

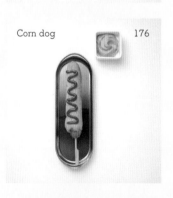

Maritozzo 178

Roll cake 182

Fruit sando 192

Satsuma imo pies 197

Daigaku imo 198

Pizza toast 204

Bread was brought to Japan by the Portuguese in the 16th century, though it wasn't until 1874 – following the isolation of Japan – that the first Japanese bun, the anpan (red bean bun), was invented. It was former samurai Kimura Yasubē who created the soft bun, filled with the Japanese wagashi (traditional sweet) staple, an (red bean). As with all Western-influenced creations, the bun was tailored to Japanese palates, and made with a yeast of fermented rice and kōji. His Tokyo bakery, Kimuraya in Ginza, still stands today.

By the 1900s, Japan was experiencing a bun bonanza, with the invention of the cream pan, melon pan and karēpan. This love affair with bread has endured. These now traditional flavours are still popular in Japan's bakeries, and in konbini the bakery section is one of its most in-demand. Partnering with Japan's leading regional bread manufacturers, konbini stock an astounding variety of breads – from soft, fluffy shokupan to classic buns, the latest trends, and collaborations with chocolate, coffee or matcha shops.

Here, we cover the classics, from Japanese favourites such as satsuma imo (sweet potato pie) and sando (sandwiches), to maritozzo and roll cake.

Shokupan — 184

Tamago sando — 187

Steamed egg omelette sando — 188

Wanpaku sando — 190

Okonomiyaki toast — 206

Japanese French toast — 208

Coppe pan — 210

Uzumaki pan — 210

Hotcake mix

Makes about 250 g (9 oz)

ホットケーキミックス

50 g (1¾ oz) shiratamako
    or glutinous rice flour
150 g (1 cup) cake flour
30 g (1 oz) sugar
2 teaspoons baking powder
½ teaspoon salt

Japan took hotcakes to literal new heights and their love for this fluffy, cloud-like, jiggly dessert continues, with dedicated hotcake shops, hotcakes in kissaten (coffee shops), and hotcake mix found in both konbini and grocery stores.

As with everything, using the right ingredients is the key to a good Japanese hotcake. A sweetened low-protein flour, a little baking powder and some starch give the hotcakes an ethereal lightness, and in our recipe, we use glutinous rice flour to give a very slightly chewy texture.

Hotcake mixes can be used for all manner of sweet and savoury applications, the most popular being donuts. The resulting donut is light and airy (rather than the denser, heavier Western counterpart), ideal for a snack that feels a bit more guilt free.

Here's our hotcake mix, followed by recipes for the fluffiest hotcakes, donuts and more.

1. If your rice flour comes in large chunks, use a food processor to blend it into a powder.

2. Whisk all the ingredients together until combined.

3. Store in an airtight container in the pantry and use as required. The mixture will keep indefinitely.

Hotcakes

ホットケーキ

1 egg yolk
1 teaspoon pure vanilla paste
1 teaspoon neutral-flavoured oil
½ teaspoon lemon juice
2 egg whites
1½ tablespoons sugar
1 tablespoon Hotcake mix
   (page 166)
1 tablespoon butter,
   plus extra to serve
maple syrup and fruit,
   to serve

Super-fluffy hotcakes are actually very easy to make at home! The key lies in whipping the egg whites and gently folding them into the batter to keep in as much air as possible. If possible, use a large, wide, non-stick frying pan – about 30 cm (12 inches) in diameter – so there's enough room to cook both hotcakes at the same time.

1. Whisk the egg yolk in a large bowl. Add the vanilla paste, oil and lemon juice and whisk to combine.

2. In a separate bowl, and using an electric mixer, whisk the egg whites until foamy, then add the sugar and whisk until stiff peaks form.

3. Using a spatula, fold the beaten egg whites into the egg yolk mixture, then sift in the hotcake mix and gently fold through until incorporated. In the bowl, divide the mixture into two even portions.

4. Heat a large lidded frying pan over medium heat and add the butter. When the butter has melted, wipe out the excess with a paper towel, then pour the divided mixture into the pan, to make two pancakes, leaving a 10 cm (4 inch) gap in between – you may need to cook in two batches.

5. Turn the heat to low, put the lid on and cook the hotcakes for 3–4 minutes. Flip the pancakes over, cover and cook for a further 3–4 minutes, until golden underneath.

6. Remove to a serving plate and serve topped with extra butter, maple syrup and fruit, as desired.

Mochi donuts

切り餅ポンデリング

Makes 6

100 g (3½ oz) shiratamako or
    glutinous rice flour
100 g (3½ oz) silken tofu
100 g (3½ oz) plain yoghurt
100 g (3½ oz) Hotcake mix
    (page 166)
neutral-flavoured oil,
    for deep-frying

A crunchy, chewy and subtly sweet donut is one of our favourite Japanese desserts, and we're hard-pressed to pass a Mister Donut shop without getting one. Our favourite is the 'pon de ring' – the photogenic garland of mochi-like donut balls. Outside Japan, it can be hard to find. Here's the recipe for your mochi donut fix.

1. If the shiratamako is in large chunks, blend it into a powder.

2. In a large bowl, whisk the tofu and yoghurt until smooth. Whisk in the shiratamako. Using clean hands, mix in the hotcake mix until a smooth dough is formed. Cover the dough with a damp cloth.

3. Divide the dough into six equal balls, then divide each ball into eight pieces, covering the dough balls with a damp cloth to prevent them drying out.

4. Cut out six 10 cm (4 inch) squares of baking paper. Arrange eight balls on each square of baking paper, in a ring shape, lightly touching each other. Allow to rest for 10 minutes.

5. Fill a large deep saucepan or deep-fryer with oil to a depth of 10 cm (4 inches) and heat to 160°C (320°F).

6. Working in batches, and leaving each donut ring on the baking paper, slide each into the oil and fry for 2 minutes, making sure the pan isn't overcrowded; don't touch the donut too much, or it will come apart. Carefully remove the paper from the oil, flip the donut and cook for another 2 minutes, until golden brown on both sides. (Be careful that the oil temperature doesn't rise too high as it will cause the donuts to puff up too much.) Remove the donuts from the oil and drain on a wire rack.

7. Glaze with one of the toppings; we recommend the vanilla glaze.

Cinnamon sugar topping
Mix 55 g (¼ cup) granulated sugar with 1 teaspoon ground cinnamon and coat the donuts in the mixture while they're still warm.

Chocolate topping
Melt 200 g (7 oz) chocolate in the microwave, or in a double boiler on the stove, then dip the tops of the donuts into the chocolate. Place on a tray and allow the chocolate to cool and harden.

Vanilla glaze topping
Mix 50 g (1¾ oz) icing (confectioners') sugar with 1½ tablespoons melted butter, 1 teaspoon lemon juice (optional) and ½ teaspoon pure vanilla paste. Dip the donuts into the glaze, place on a tray and allow the glaze to harden.

Old-fashioned donuts

オールドファッションドーナツ

Makes 6

200 g (7 oz) Hotcake mix
(page 166)
1 egg
1 tablespoon sugar
1 tablespoon neutral-flavoured
oil, plus extra for deep-frying

A crunchy, cake-style donut that's extremely easy to throw together. The cratered exterior provides extra crunch as well as more surface area for toppings to stick to.

1. Place the hotcake mix in a large bowl. Crack the egg into the middle. Place the sugar and oil in the middle and gently bring all the ingredients together using a spatula or pastry scraper. Try not to work it too much, or it may become tough. When it becomes a dough, turn it out onto a bench, then flatten with the palm of your hand into a rough rectangle.

2. Fold the dough in half to make a square. Repeat this step two more times, to create flaky layers in the dough.

3. Roll the dough out into a 20 cm (8 inch) square, wrap in plastic wrap and rest in the refrigerator for 30 minutes.

4. Fill a large deep saucepan or deep-fryer with oil to a depth of 10 cm (4 inches) and heat to 160°C (320°F). Set a wire rack over a tray for draining, and have ready a 7 cm (2¾ inch) and a 3 cm (1¼ inch) cutter.

5. Roll the dough out to 1 cm (½ inch) thick. Using the cutters, cut out 7 cm (2¾ inch) rounds, then cut a 3 cm (1¼ inch) hole in the middle, placing the donuts on individual sheets of baking paper. Re-form the left-over dough into a ball, roll out to 1 cm (½ inch) thick again and cut out more donuts. Repeat until all the dough is used up.

6. Using a 5 cm (2 inch) cutter, make a shallow indent in the top of each donut. Using a skewer, trace the outline of the indent to create a rough circle on the top of the dough to make the distinctive old-fashioned double-ring look, and to make the exterior more crunchy.

7. Deep-fry the donuts in batches for 2 minutes on each side, or until golden, then transfer to the wire rack to drain and cool.

8. Glaze with any of the toppings on page 170. We recommend the cinnamon sugar or chocolate toppings.

Pound cake

パウンドケーキ

1 lemon
50 g (1¾ oz) butter
50 ml (1¾ fl oz) milk
1 egg
75 g (2¾ oz) sugar,
    plus extra for the syrup
150 g (5½ oz) Hotcake mix
    (page 166)
50 g (1¾ oz) icing
    (confectioners') sugar
dried flower petals,
    to garnish (optional)

Hotcake mix makes very light pound cakes, which are popular in Japan.

Sold in French–Japanese bakeries, patisseries and konbinis (as single slices), these light yet rich cakes come in flavours of matcha, rich chocolate, sakura, butter and lemon.

This recipe is for a lemon pound cake, which has an addictive citrusy tang.

1. Preheat the oven to 170°C (340°F). Grease a 15 cm (6 inch) loaf (bar) tin with oil and line with baking paper.

2. Zest and juice the lemon, keeping the zest and juice separate.

3. Place the butter and milk in a microwave-safe bowl and microwave in 15-second bursts until the butter is melted. Add the egg, sugar and lemon zest and whisk until combined. Pour in the hotcake mix and whisk until smooth.

4. Pour the batter into the loaf tin. Gently drop the tin on a tea towel on the bench to remove any air bubbles and smooth the top, then bake for 10 minutes.

5. Remove from the oven and, using a sharp knife, draw a line down the centre of the cake. This step creates a nice split in the centre of the loaf.

6. Bake for another 30 minutes, or until a skewer inserted in the centre comes out clean. Remove from the oven.

7. Mix half the lemon juice with an equal weight of sugar until the sugar dissolves. Poke a few holes in the cake using a skewer, then pour the lemon syrup into the cake. Leave the cake to cool in the tin.

8. Mix the remaining lemon juice with the icing sugar. You're after a consistency similar to thick cream, so add a little more icing sugar to make it thicker, or more water to thin it, if required.

9. Remove the cake from the tin and place on a wire rack set over a tray. Pour the lemon icing over and sprinkle with dried flowers, if desired. Let the cake cool fully before cutting and serving. The cake is best consumed within 3 days.

Corn dog

アメリカンドッグ

neutral-flavoured oil,
    for deep-frying
4 frankfurters
ketchup and mustard,
    to serve

Batter
100 g (3½ oz) Hotcake mix
    (page 166)
50 g (1¾ oz) cornmeal or polenta
80 ml (⅓ cup) milk
1 egg

Hotcake mix isn't only for sweets. Corn dogs – the matsuri (Japanese festival) favourite of a cornmeal-battered hotdog on a stick – can also be made with hotcake mix. It puffs up nicely, and the sweetness works well with the saltiness of the sausage.

1. Fill a large deep saucepan or deep-fryer with oil to a depth of 10 cm (4 inches) and heat to 170°C (340°F).

2. Insert a wooden or metal skewer lengthways through the middle of each frankfurter, leaving a handle at one end.

3. In a large bowl, mix together the batter ingredients.

4. Working in batches, dip the frankfurters in the batter, allowing the excess to drain off, then gently lower into the oil. Cook, turning regularly with wooden chopsticks, for about 5 minutes, until golden all over. Drain on a wire rack and allow to cool for 2–3 minutes, until the handle is room temperature.

5. Serve warm, with ketchup and mustard.

Maritozzo

マリトッツォ

3 eggs
30 ml (1 fl oz) milk,
    plus extra for brushing
250 g (1⅔ cups) bread flour
2½ teaspoons bread improver
7 g (2 teaspoons) instant yeast
30 g (1 oz) sugar
½ teaspoon salt
60 g (2 oz) butter,
    at room temperature

Filling

120 ml (4 fl oz) cream
80 g (2¾ oz) mascarpone
1½ tablespoons sugar
1 teaspoon pure vanilla paste
    or natural vanilla extract
your choice of fruits, chocolate
    or nuts, to fill and decorate

These attractive Italian sweet buns have taken over Japanese bakeries – and the bakery section of konbinis. The soft brioche-like bread pairs well with the high-quality Japanese dairy and fruits, in a similar way to Japanese shortcake or fruit sando (page 192), two other Japanese favourites.

What differentiates maritozzo from the other baked sweets is a richer bread that holds up to crunchier toppings such as chocolate chips and nuts.

For the lightest texture, these are best eaten the day they are made.

1. Crack the eggs into a small bowl, pour in the milk and whisk to combine.

2. In a large bowl, mix together the flour, bread improver and yeast. Add the sugar and salt and mix again. Add the milk and egg mixture and mix using a pastry scraper until combined. Finally, add the butter and use the scraper to cut it in until mostly homogenous. If the dough is very firm, add more milk, a teaspoon at a time, to get the correct consistency. It should be quite sticky at first.

3. Mix using a stand mixer or by hand on the bench until the dough is smooth and elastic, about 10 minutes. Place in a greased bowl, cover with plastic wrap and leave to rise for 1 hour in a warm place, or until doubled in size.

4. Knock out the air and divide the dough into eight equal balls, about 60 g (2 oz) each. Cover with a damp cloth and allow to rest on the bench for 15 minutes.

5. Line a baking tray with baking paper. Press the air out of the dough balls and shape into rounds. Place on the lined baking tray, leaving a 10 cm (4 inch) gap between each. Cover and leave to rest for 1 hour.

6. Preheat the oven to 200°C (400°F).

7. Brush the buns with extra milk and place in the oven. Turn the heat down to 180°C (350°F). Bake for 16 minutes, or until the buns sound hollow when tapped. Remove from the oven and allow to cool.

8. To make the filling, use an electric mixer to whip the cream, mascarpone, sugar and vanilla to stiff peaks.

9. When the buns are cool, cut them like a hot dog bun, on an angle. Place some of your chosen fruits, chocolate or nuts inside, then fill with the sweet cream, smoothing out the cream. Arrange a little more of your chosen ingredient on the cream and eat!

The Premium Roll Cake

THE ROLL CAKE: A JAPANESE classic that's always in vogue. Soft, fluffy, filled with cream. Perhaps too much cream if you aren't Japanese, until you have a taste. It's ethereal, what biting into a cloud must feel like. Light, airy, with just a slight sweetness from the milk or whatever fruit they have decided to flavour it with. The perfect foil to the soft, eggy sweetness of the sponge.

Under the glittering glass cases of the depachika (department food halls, 'depa' being short for 'department', and 'chika' meaning 'underground'), this is a prized cake beautifully presented – the type of purchase you'd make to bring as a gift to a dinner party host, impress the partner's parents, or to celebrate a special occasion with the family.

The catch? Roll cakes are sold as rolls. And in Japan's cities, where an increasing number of people live alone, a roll cake isn't something they can finish on their own.

It was this thought that spurred Lawson's Premium Roll Cake – their best-selling item. Until then, konbini desserts weren't known for being particularly good. The best cakes and desserts with the prized 'nama kurimu' (raw cream) were found in the specialty cake stores in depachika, while konbini versions had a reputation for having cream that was stiff and hard. And so, the Lawson team developed a nama cream that could hold its own. They decided to create a point of difference – to purvey a slice of roll cake for the solo diner, turned on its side so it could be easily eaten with a spoon. The rest is history. The premium roll cake secured Lawson's reputation as the konbini chain with the outstanding desserts.

The Lawson premium roll cake

A perfect oval roll without the characteristic spiral. Its texture and airy, pure white mousse could convince you this came from a premium cake shop. Halo-level, dinner-party worthy, for under 200 yen at the konbini.

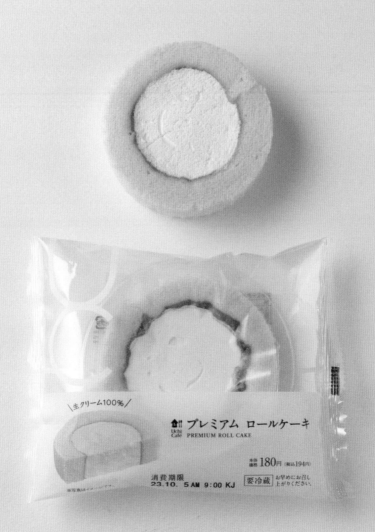

Roll cake

ロールケーキ

4 eggs
100 g (3½ oz) sugar, divided
    into 65 g (2¼ oz) and
    35 g (1¼ oz)
40 ml (1¼ fl oz) neutral-
    flavoured oil
65 ml (2¼ fl oz) boiling water
80 g (2¾ oz) cake flour
½ teaspoon baking powder

Filling

250 g (9 oz) strawberries,
    washed (optional)
300 ml (10½ fl oz) cream
30 g (1 oz) sugar

One of the konbini's most popular dessert items, the roll cake comes in many styles, from Lawson's – which features a thick cake encircling a dollop of light cream – to spiral cakes with fine, paper-thin layers of cake and cream.

These swirl-style cakes come in flavours of matcha, chocolate or coffee, often in partnership with renowned matcha tea shops, chocolate makers and coffee roasteries. Lawson's coffee roll cake is made with coffee from local Tokyo roaster and coffee shop, Sarutahiko Coffee.

This recipe is for the thicker style of cake, so you can enjoy the soft cake and fresh cream separately or together, with every bite a different flavour and texture. You can also add fruit to the centre. We've used strawberries, but any fruit of a similar size will work, such as grapes, figs or kiwifruit.

1. Preheat the oven to 180°C (350°F). Line a 25 x 35 cm (10 x 14 inch) roll cake tin or lipped baking tray with baking paper. Grease the baking paper with baking spray or neutral-flavoured oil.

2. Separate the egg yolks and egg whites.

3. Whisk the egg whites with the 35 g (1¼ oz) of sugar to firm peaks and place in the fridge.

4. In a separate bowl, whisk the egg yolks and the 65 g (2¼ oz) of sugar until doubled in volume. Stream in the oil while whisking, then add the boiling water and whisk well.

5. Sift in the flour and baking powder and fold through with a spatula, then fold in the beaten egg whites.

6. Pour into the roll cake tin and smooth the surface. Drop the tin from a height of 10 cm (4 inches) onto the bench to remove any large bubbles, then bake for 12–15 minutes, until the cake is golden and a skewer inserted into the centre comes out clean.

7. Meanwhile, if using strawberries, cut the tops off. If some are very wide, use a round cutter to remove the sides so they are mostly uniform in diameter. Place on a paper towel in the fridge to absorb any excess water.

8. Remove the cake from the oven. Grease a sheet of baking paper, then place it, greased side down, on top of the cake and turn the cake out onto a cooling rack. Allow to cool to room temperature, which will take 20–30 minutes.

9. When the cake is cool, make the filling by whipping the cream and sugar to firm peaks.

10. Remove the top sheet of baking paper from the cake. Trim the cake to make the edges straight and remove any overcooked edges. Spread the cream evenly over the top, leaving a 2 cm (¾ inch) border on one long edge.

11. If using strawberries, place them in a horizontal line in the centre of the cream. Press them in lightly so they don't move when being rolled.

12. With the cream-free end away from you, take the closest side and roll the cake up tightly, using the baking paper to aid you. Make the roll quite tight, so the cream fills in any air gaps.

13. Still rolled inside the baking paper, carefully transfer the cake to a plate. Refrigerate for at least 6 hours, or overnight, to set.

14. Take off the baking paper, slice the cake and serve. The cake is best consumed within 2 days.

Shokupan

食パン

220 g (8 oz) flour
165 ml (5½ fl oz) milk
50 g (1¾ oz) sugar
2 teaspoons salt
4 g (1¼ teaspoons) dried yeast
60 g (2 oz) butter, at room
    temperature, diced

Preferment
220 g (8 oz) flour
165 ml (5½ fl oz) water
2.5 g (¾ teaspoon) dried yeast

The base for many sweet and savoury treats in Japan is the soft, pillowy shokupan – a type of fluffy bread that sits somewhere between a brioche and Western white bread. It has a wonderful flavour from the milk and butter, without being too rich. The bread comes apart in long, soft shreds, which is unique to shokupan and its folding process, making it chewier and more satisfying than white bread.

Shokupan is best when it's fresh and used in sandwiches. If it's two or more days old, then toast, French toast or pizza toast are the way to go. Beyond 5 days, shred it up to make nama panko (fresh Japanese breadcrumbs) for crumbing tonkatsu (page 156).

You'll need a 2.8 litre (95 fl oz) lidded loaf tin for this recipe, and you'll need to start a day ahead.

1. Start by making the preferment. Mix the ingredients together, then cover and leave for 12–16 hours at room temperature, until doubled in size.

2. The next day, put the preferment in the bowl of a stand mixer. Add all the remaining ingredients except the butter. Using a dough hook, knead on low speed for 5 minutes.

3. Scrape down the side of the bowl, add the butter and knead for another 10 minutes, or until the dough is very elastic, scraping down the side of the bowl every 2 minutes.

4. When the dough is ready, scrape down the side of the bowl again. Cover and leave to rest in a warm place for 1 hour, or until the dough has doubled in size.

5. Turn the dough out onto a clean bench and divide into three even pieces. Form each piece into a smooth ball, then cover and leave to rest for 20 minutes.

6. Meanwhile, lightly grease the inside of a 2.8 litre (95 fl oz) lidded loaf tin with neutral-flavoured oil.

7. Lightly flour your bench. Turn one rested dough ball over onto the bench so the smooth side faces down. Using your hands or a rolling pin, stretch the dough to roughly the size of an A4 sheet of paper, or about 20 x 30 cm (8–12 inches). With the longer edge in front of you, fold the left side of the dough over two-thirds of the dough. Press down to remove any large air bubbles, then fold the right side all the way over to the left edge.

8. Take the top of the dough with both hands, then tightly roll from top to bottom to create a log. Seal the excess dough by pinching it together, then place, seal side down, in the loaf tin. Repeat with the remaining two dough balls.

9. Slide the lid on the loaf tin and leave in a warm place for 1 hour, or until the dough has doubled in size.

10. Preheat the oven to 180°C (350°F). Bake the loaf for 20 minutes, then turn the oven down to 165°C (330°F) and bake for another 15 minutes.

11. Remove the loaf from the oven, carefully remove the lid and turn the loaf out onto a cooling rack. Allow to cool for 30 minutes before slicing.

Sando

サンド

Japan's konbini sandwiches have something of a legendary reputation – fluffy (not soggy!) bread, perfectly buttered or creamed, and filled with premium ingredients. No trip to Japan is complete without one. Especially the tamago (egg salad) sandwich, which can be rearranged by slipping Famichiki's fried chicken cutlet or Lawson's Karaage-Kun (chicken nuggets) within.

One of the secrets lies in the balance of toppings and consideration to texture. Sando are typically filled with soft ingredients that fit in a mouthful, so they don't drag all of the fillings out.

Tamago sando

卵サンド

3 eggs, at room temperature
1 tablespoon butter,
    at room temperature
1 teaspoon Japanese mustard paste
1 tablespoon mayonnaise
½ teaspoon rice vinegar
¼ teaspoon salt
5 grinds of black pepper
2 thick slices of Shokupan
    (page 184)

1. Bring a pot of water to the boil, carefully add the eggs, then boil the eggs for 9 minutes. Drain and cool in iced water, then peel and set aside.

2. In a small bowl, mix together the butter and mustard paste.

3. Cut two of the eggs in half, then scoop the yolks into a bowl. Add the mayonnaise, mashing the yolks until the mixture is smooth. Stir in the rice vinegar, salt and pepper.

4. Dice the egg whites from the sliced eggs and add to the yolks, mixing well.

5. Spread the butter mixture on the two slices of bread. Cut the remaining egg in half, then lay the egg halves side by side in the centre of one of the slices. Spoon the mayonnaise mixture over and spread evenly, leaving a 1 cm (½ inch) border at the edge.

6. Place the other slice of bread on top, buttered side down, then wrap tightly in plastic wrap. You'll be cutting the sandwich into three fingers, so use a marker to draw two vertical lines on the wrap where the halved eggs are, so you can later cut through to reveal the yolks.

7. Refrigerate for 30 minutes to firm up.

8. Cutting through the plastic wrap, slice off the crusts, then slice along your marked lines to cut your sando into three fingers. Remove the wrap and serve.

Steamed egg omelette sando

Serves 1

蒸しタマゴサンド

1 tablespoon mayonnaise
½ teaspoon mustard
2 thick slices of Shokupan
(page 184)
1 slice of American
cheese (optional)

Omelette

3 eggs
3 tablespoons milk or water
1 tablespoon mirin
1 teaspoon usukuchi soy sauce
1 teaspoon sugar
½ teaspoon salt
½ teaspoon dashi powder
½ teaspoon potato starch

A simpler version of the tamago sando that only requires the microwave. The soft, warm omelette is delicious as a filling on its own, though you can add chopped vegetables, such as onion and capsicum (bell pepper), for more flavour and texture. A slice of cheese also works well.

1. Grease a small microwave-proof dish with butter or neutral-flavoured oil. In a small bowl, whisk all the omelette ingredients together, pour into the microwave dish and cover.

2. Microwave at 600 watts for 1½ minutes. Whisk to break up any curds, scrape the sides of the dish, then microwave for a further 1½ minutes.

3. Meanwhile, spread the mayonnaise and mustard on both slices of bread and season with salt and pepper.

4. Slide the omelette onto one slice of bread, place the slice of cheese on top (if using), then the other slice of bread on top. Wrap tightly in plastic wrap and leave for 5 minutes.

5. Cut off the crusts, then cut in half and serve.

Wanpaku sando

わんぱくサンド

1 egg, at room temperature
½ tomato
½ cooked chicken breast,
    from the Salad chicken
    recipe on page 244
salt and pepper
1 tablespoon mayonnaise
½ teaspoon mustard
2 thick slices of Shokupan
    (page 184)
1 slice of cheese
2 lettuce leaves, washed
¼ carrot, peeled and shredded
½ avocado, flesh sliced

Wanpaku sando, or 'naughty sandwich', is so large and extreme it's almost comical. But it's full of healthy vegetables and low-fat protein to fuel busy people through the day. What makes this sandwich Japanese is the cutting techniques, the layering of ingredients, and the use of colours. Feel free to add or remove toppings as you like. The limit is your imagination.

When preparing the ingredients, dry them thoroughly on paper towels to prevent the bread becoming soggy and the ingredients slipping around.

Other savoury sandwich ideas
Potato salad (page 123)
    and crispy bacon
Any croquette (pages 60–67)
    with shredded cabbage,
    tonkatsu sauce,
    and/or mayonnaise
Torimeshi (page 26)
    and tamago (page 39)

1. Bring a pot of water to the boil, carefully add the egg, then boil for 8 minutes. Drain and place in a bowl of cold water. When cooled to room temperature, peel the egg.

2. Slice the tomato and chicken 1 cm (½ inch) thick. Season with salt and pepper and place on paper towel to absorb the excess moisture.

3. Mix the mayonnaise with the mustard. Season with salt and pepper.

4. Working on a large sheet of baking paper, spread the mayonnaise mixture on both slices of bread. Place the cheese on one slice, then the lettuce, tomato, chicken, egg, carrot and avocado. The key is to keep most of the toppings around the centre, like a mountain.

5. Sandwich the second slice on top and wrap very tightly with the baking paper. Allow to rest for 10 minutes, then cut in half and serve.

Fruit sando

フルーツサンド

5 strawberries (small to medium
   in size), or ½ cup mixed fruit
   (peeled and cut to the size
   of small strawberries)
60 g (2 oz) mascarpone
60 g (2 oz) cream
1½ tablespoons sugar
2 thick slices of Shokupan
   (page 184)

Japanese love their fruit sandwiches — from strawberries to Shine Muscat grapes, kiwifruit and mikan (mandarin), or a medley of these. Soft, fluffy and light, fruit sando are like biting into clouds of lightly sweetened cream and tangy fruits, with a gentle sweetness from the bread.

1. Clean or peel the fruit as necessary, then set aside to dry on paper towel in the refrigerator. Place the mascarpone in a bowl and massage with a spatula to soften it.

2. Using an electric mixer, whisk the cream and sugar to soft peaks, then add the mascarpone and whisk to firm peaks.

3. Lay a slice of bread on a large square of plastic wrap and spread with a layer of cream. Place three pieces of fruit on the cream in a diagonal line, then another two fruit pieces in the empty space on each side of the diagonal line. Use the remaining cream to fill in the gaps between the fruit and cover everything in cream.

4. Place the other slice of bread on top and wrap tightly in plastic wrap. Use a marker to draw a diagonal where you've placed your line of fruit.

5. Refrigerate for at least 3 hours, or overnight.

6. Keeping the plastic wrap on, cut along the line through the sandwich to divide it in two, then cut off the crusts. Remove the wrap and serve.

Going Local

IT'S AUTUMN, WHICH MEANS SWEET POTATO SEASON – the humble tuber finding its way into stores as caramelised sweet potato chips, sweet potato pan (bread), sweet potato ice cream, steamed sweet potato and... 'We sell it on its own too,' Mochimaru Ken-san says.

We remember alighting at a small station in Nagano – a wooden structure for a train platform, manned by two staff. Neatly displayed outside was a table full of baskets of local vegetables – root, leafy and fruit. An obasan (grandmother) wandered by and studied them carefully. She picked up some, called out to the staff member, then placed the cash into his gloved hand. It was apparently a normal, everyday exchange in these parts, and now in some rural konbinis too.

Lawson is the only konbini chain to form a collaboration with 17 farms – each independently owned, but exclusive suppliers for the company. More than a strategic movement in terms of supply chain control, it also gives Lawson the chance to fly the locally made flag – 'Japan-grown' and 'Japan-made' being an important consideration and a reassuring symbol of quality for the Japanese.

The farmers are assured of a steady stream of business, and, in turn, Lawson are able to nominate the produce they want. Scattered throughout Japan, with each growing a different vegetable or fruit, the farms allow Lawson to develop different ranges that showcase the local meibutsu (regional specialty) – something the prefectures in Japan are very proud of.

The vegetables find their way into salads and chips – made by Calbee for Lawson featuring locally grown sweet potato (from Lawson Farm Chiba), carrot and squash. In autumn and winter, the sweet potatoes are also stone-grilled and served in select stores. Fruits are turned into delicious little cubes of fruit jelly in Kyoho grape, peach (from Lawson Farm Yamanashi) and pineapple flavours, or infused into the cream in their dessert choux. Even the milk in Lawson's coffees is local – sourced from dairy farms in the area.

There's a sense of regional pride in these home-grown offerings – and for the visiting konbini hunter, a very accessible way to sample local specialties.

Sweet potato

薩摩芋パイ

Sweet potato stars in both savoury and sweet dishes in Japan, and is much loved in autumn, when it comes into season. Travelling through the regional countryside, you will find small carts or stalls selling the slow-cooked potato (yaki-imo), steamed or grilled until the flesh is sweet and almost custardy. Yaki-imo have made their way into konbini too, sold alongside sweet potato chips, puddings, soft-serves and beer.

Kawagoe is known as the home of sweet potato, with many different sweet potato treats sold in its historic streets.

Satsuma imo pies

さつまいもパイ

80 g (2¾ oz) raisins
2 tablespoons rum
500 g (1 lb 2 oz) purple
    sweet potato or regular
    sweet potato
1 egg
1 tablespoon butter,
    at room temperature
1 tablespoon sugar
1 tablespoon honey
½ teaspoon ground cinnamon
½ teaspoon ground nutmeg
½ teaspoon salt
2 frozen puff pastry
    sheets, just thawed

Egg wash
1 egg
1 tablespoon milk

Glaze
230 g (1 cup) sugar
185 ml (¾ cup) water

This satsuma imo (sweet potato) pie was inspired by our travels to Kawagoe. The creamy sweet potato filling, encased in puff pastry, is punctuated by bursts of rum and sweetness from the soaked raisins, while the cinnamon and nutmeg provide a warming note.

You can also bake the sweet potato as in the recipe below and eat it on its own for a healthy dessert (like those sold by yaki-imo carts in Japan), or serve it with ice cream to make it less so.

1. The day before, marinate the raisins in the rum and set aside to infuse.

2. Preheat the oven to 160°C (320°F). Wrap the whole sweet potato in foil and bake for 3 hours, or until soft. Allow to cool enough to handle, then remove the skin and mash the flesh in a large bowl until mostly smooth. You should have around 350 g (12½ oz) sweet potato.

3. Stir the egg, butter, sugar, honey, cinnamon, nutmeg and salt through the mashed sweet potato. Mix in the soaked raisins and rum.

4. Turn the oven up to 200°C (400°F). Whisk the egg wash ingredients together.

5. Keeping the puff pastry as cold as possible, cut each sheet into eight rectangles, measuring about 6.25 x 12.5 cm (2½ x 5 inches). If possible, use a pastry wheel to cut half the pastry rectangles with a lattice pattern. Top the remaining pastry rectangles with the sweet potato mixture, leaving a 1 cm (½ inch) border. Brush the edges with the egg wash and top with the lattice sheets, pressing them into the bottom sheet. Brush again with the egg wash.

6. Bake for 25 minutes, or until light golden brown. Meanwhile, make the glaze by boiling together the sugar and water.

7. Brush the pastries with the glaze, then bake for a further 5 minutes. The pies are best served warm. They will also keep in an airtight container in the fridge for up to 5 days, and can either be eaten cold or reheated in a 160°C (320°F) oven for 8–10 minutes.

Daigaku imo

大学芋

500 g (1 lb 2 oz) purple
    sweet potato or regular
    sweet potato
neutral-flavoured oil,
    for deep-frying
60 g (2 oz) sugar
2 tablespoons water
1 tablespoon soy sauce
1 tablespoon roasted black
    sesame seeds

In the early 1900s, Japanese university students subsisted on this dish as it was inexpensive and kept them full during their long days of studying. The dish now bears the name 'daigaku imo', or 'university sweet potato', in their honour.

It consists of crunchy, fried sweet potato candied in a caramel made slightly salty from soy sauce – an addictive treat when sweet potatoes are at their best.

1. Cut the sweet potato into 2.5 cm (1 inch) square chunks, keeping each piece roughly the same size so they cook at the same time.

2. Prepare two steamer baskets by lining them with baking paper, and punching a few holes in the paper to let the steam through.

3. Prepare a pot with boiling water for the steamer baskets to sit on. Place the sweet potato in the steamer baskets and steam for 10 minutes, or until almost cooked but still keeping their shape. Remove from the heat and allow to cool for 5 minutes.

4. Meanwhile, fill a large deep saucepan or deep-fryer with oil to a depth of 10 cm (4 inches) and heat to 170° C (340° F).

5. Deep-fry the sweet potatoes, in batches if necessary, for about 5 minutes, until golden brown. Drain on paper towel.

6. In a frying pan, dissolve the sugar in the water over medium heat. When the mixture turns golden brown, turn the heat to low and stir in the soy sauce. Add the sweet potato and stir to coat, then turn off the heat.

7. Transfer the sweet potato to a serving bowl. Sprinkle with the sesame seeds and serve.

Avatars, deep-freeze technology & Konbinis of the future

IN THE BUSY CENTRE OF TOKYO, filled with younger businessmen and women dipping in and out of konbinis and going about their everyday life, it can be hard to envision Japan as an ageing society. The city is buzzing, thriving; the train stations overflowing in the morning and evening rush; queues of couples, colleagues and friends waiting patiently outside kissaten, restaurants and dessert parlours from Shinjuku to Ginza.

But already, Japan's konbinis are facing challenges, with fewer drivers for deliveries and fewer staff available to work in stores.

Travelling through Japan's towns, sometimes just a train stop or two from cities, the shuttered shops, vacant streets, limited buses and rusting bridges make the gradual depopulation of rural areas even more apparent. In Kamasaki Onsen, the remote onsen town we talk about at the start of the book, there were no konbinis: the closest was a NewDays in the nearest Shinkansen station – a favourite of ours since they tend to be stocked with local craft ware, meibutsu (famous local goods) and omiyage (souvenirs).

Away from the shining lights of Osaka, Tokyo and bigger city hubs, the fading away of suburban and rural Japan is something visible and tangible. No younger high school students looking for an arubaito (part-time job), much less the near-impossible task of keeping a konbini open 24/7.

Enter the avatars, found in Green Lawson, launched as a testing ground for an avatar-only operation in Toshima ward, Tokyo. A solo staff member exists – to cook and stock the shelves – but the rest of the konbini experience is carried out purely through Aoi (female) and Sorato (male) avatars designed (of course!) in the style of anime characters, ready to help through a screen if needed.

There are actually humans behind these avatars – individuals with social anxiety, disabilities, and care-giving or child-rearing responsibilities, based locally or in other areas of Japan, who take turns manning the system. Through a microphone and cameras on the screens in-store, they assist the customers – a pathway that gives them a place in society, and a solution to the staff shortages konbinis face.

To attempt something like this in another country would be unthinkable, given that it operates on a system of absolute trust. But in a place like Japan, where society still prides itself on honesty and integrity, it may well be the answer.

Deep-freeze technology also features in Lawson's futuristic lab – frozen foods from onigiri to okonomiyaki and takoyaki, popular Japanese snacks of korokke (croquettes), menchi katsu (meat cutlets), gyoza, shumai, gyutan (beef tongue), tsukune and kalbi, to pasta and gratin. (Ah... the perfect end after a long day of work, to pair with beer... preferably at a kotatsu on the living room floor.)

We also found basashi (horse sashimi) nestled next to gyu yukke, a Japanese adaptation of the Korean dish 'yukhoe': seasoned beef tartare with raw egg yolk and usually a splash of shoyu and mirin.

The former – known by the evocative name of 'sakura niku' or 'cherry blossom meat' on Japanese menus – traces its origins back to Kumamoto almost 400 years ago, during the warring period between Japanese samurai. War horses were first eaten when rations ran low, a practice that spread to other parts of Japan once the war ended. By the Edo area, horses were seen as a nutritious food with medicinal properties, and continue to be consumed today. It is worth noting that horse is still eaten in parts of Europe as well.

But if frozen horse sashimi is unusual, the konbini freezer doesn't stop there. In 2023, Japan developed a technology to flash-freeze sashimi and sushi. In a country with bountiful access to fresh fish, whether in the markets or depachika, and where chefs behind smooth hinoki counters carve prized fish into tantalising bite-sized slivers for those willing to pay the price each night, freezing what can be considered a highly delicate national dish feels a touch sacrilegious.

Interestingly, however, this technology was embraced by a respected fishmonger, Tōshin Suisan, which has been in the business for over 70 years, and has branches in high-end depachika including Ginza's storied Mitsukoshi department store.

Tōshin Suisan sell their fish as frozen sashimi and nigirizushi that can be shipped anywhere in Japan. The sashimi and nigiri are 'flash-frozen' using a novel alcohol and liquid-freezing method that preserves their quality, colour, cell structure, umami and moisture. The same technology also proved successful with the shari (rice), which retained its fluffiness and flavour when defrosted.

Lawson has cut no corners, partnering with a company that offers the same technology for their frozen sashimi, nigiri and yukke. For sashimi and sushi lovers, this currently provides access to a supply of sea bream sashimi and amberjack sashimi in their local konbinis, flash-frozen when the fish are at their seasonal peak.

But more than just a bid to break new frontiers, the frozen sashimi also represents the new turn Lawson and other konbini chains have had to take: investing in frozen product development to combat fewer deliveries while still offering a plethora of variety.

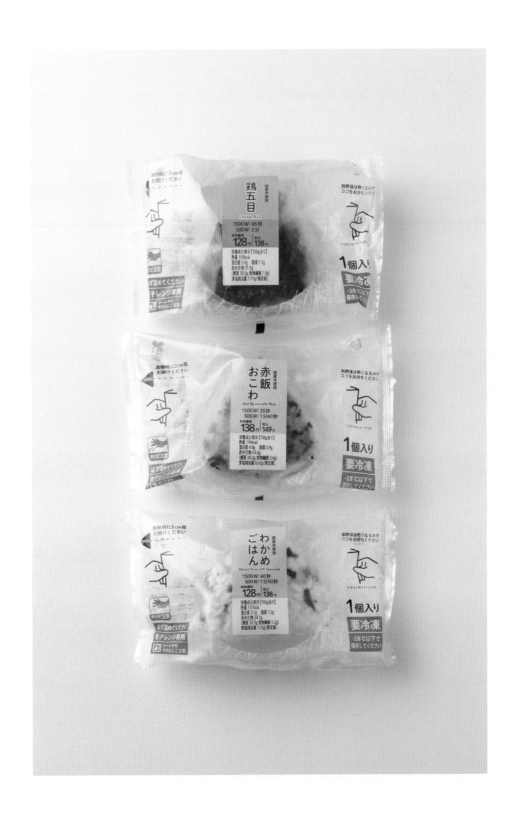

Pizza toast

ピザトースト

2 thick slices of Shokupan
    (page 184)
2 tablespoons ketchup
⅛ onion, thinly sliced
¼ capsicum (bell pepper),
    thinly sliced into rounds
    and seeded
2 slices of ham or bacon, diced
35 g (¼ cup) grated melting
    cheese, such as mozzarella
1 tablespoon mayonnaise

The pizza toast was born in Japan's traditional coffee dens, the kissaten (喫茶店). Most kissa don't have kitchens, and pizza toast – a simple dish of thickly sliced shokupan topped with tomato paste (concentrated purée), capsicum, cheese and other toppings – became the de facto accompaniment to the hand-drip and siphon coffee the kissa specialise in, as all it requires for cooking is a toaster oven.

Naturally, the pizza toast found its way into konbini, even making an appearance in the hot box section (on the konbini counter) as pizzaman (ピザマン – the 'man' here being a Chinese bun). All the ingredients can also be easily picked up in a konbini, and put together in minutes.

1. Preheat an overhead grill (broiler) and toast the bread slices on one side.

2. On the untoasted side, use a sharp knife to cut a three-by-three grid halfway through the bread. (Score the bread into thirds, running horizontally across the bread, and from top to bottom.) This technique provides maximum crustiness and pull-apart-ness.

3. Spread the ketchup on the untoasted side and grind on some pepper. Top with the onion, capsicum, ham, and then the cheese. Zig-zag with mayonnaise and place back under the grill for about 2 minutes, until the cheese has melted.

4. Allow to rest for 1 minute, then serve.

Okonomiyaki toast

お好み焼きトースト

2 thick slices of Shokupan
   (page 184)
2 cabbage leaves,
   finely shredded
2 slices of ham, sliced into
   1 cm (½ inch) strips
2 eggs
35 g (¼ cup) grated melting
   cheese, such as mozzarella
2 tablespoons mayonnaise
2 tablespoons okonomiyaki sauce
2 pinches of katsuobushi
   (bonito flakes)
2 pinches of aonori
2 teaspoons benishoga
   (pickled ginger)

A variation of pizza toast (page 204), using the flavours of okonomiyaki (page 142). Less common than pizza toast, but delicious all the same, it's perfect for those looking for a more Japanese-flavoured snack.

1. Preheat an overhead grill (broiler) and toast the bread slices on one side.

2. On the untoasted side, use a sharp knife to cut a three-by-three grid halfway through the bread. (Score the bread into thirds, running horizontally across the bread, and from top to bottom.) This technique provides maximum crustiness and pull-apart-ness.

3. In a microwave-safe bowl, microwave the cabbage for 1 minute, or until softened. Allow to cool slightly.

4. Spread the ham over the untoasted side of each bread slice. Divide the cabbage between the two and make a well in the centre. Crack an egg into each well and cover with the cheese. Toast under the grill for 5–7 minutes, until the egg is cooked to your liking.

5. Remove from the grill and drizzle with the mayonnaise and okonomiyaki sauce. Serve sprinkled with the bonito flakes, aonori and pickled ginger.

Japanese French toast

フレンチトースト

4 eggs
200 ml (7 fl oz) milk
50 g (1¾ oz) sugar
½ teaspoon pure vanilla paste
4 slices of white bread
    (preferably Shokupan,
    page 184), cut 3 cm
    (1¼ inches) thick
1 tablespoon butter
fruit, maple syrup and
    extra butter, to serve

Soft, custardy French toast is just one of the dishes Japan took and made into the best version of itself. You'll find it sold in the bakery section of konbini, but we love making it fresh (with drip coffee) on weekend mornings.

The key is the long, overnight soak in the custard mixture, so no parts of the bread are dry, making it creamy and luscious all the way through.

French toast can also be made ahead of time, then microwaved; it won't be as light or have the little crispy toasted bits on the outside, and will have more of a set custard.

1. The night before, mix together the eggs, milk, sugar and vanilla paste. Pour into a deep tray that will fit all the bread. Cut the crusts off the bread. Soak the bread in the milk mixture, turning the slices over a few times and spooning the mixture over the bread. The bread is best soaked for 12 hours.

2. The next morning, carefully remove the bread from the egg mixture and drain well on a wire rack. Discard the egg mixture. Turn the oven on low, about 60°C (140°F), and place two plates inside to keep warm.

3. Melt the butter in a large lidded, non-stick frying pan over medium heat. When the butter is foaming and completely melted, add the bread.

4. Turn the heat down to low, then cover and cook for 5 minutes. Remove the lid and turn the slices over. The bread should be golden brown on the cooked side; if not, turn the heat up slightly.

5. Cover and cook for another 5 minutes, or until a skewer inserted into the centre comes out hot, and both sides of the bread are golden brown and crisp. Turn the heat up to medium and quickly cook the four remaining edges of toast to evenly brown.

6. Serve the toast on the warmed plates, with extra butter, fruit and maple syrup.

VARIATION

Ham & cheese French toast

ハムチーズフレンチトースト

4 eggs
200 ml (7 fl oz) milk
50 g (1¾ oz) sugar
4 slices of white bread
    (preferably Shokupan,
    page 184), cut 1.5 cm
    (½ inch) thick
1 tablespoon butter
2 slices of melting cheese,
    such as Comté or Gruyère
2 slices of ham
maple syrup, to serve (optional)

Sandwiching French toast with salty ham and cheese balances the sweetness beautifully – in the same way that bacon pairs well with pancakes. This version is otherwise very similar to the Japanese French toast above, except the bread is sliced more thinly and requires a much shorter soaking time.

1. In a bowl, mix together the eggs, milk and sugar. Pour into a deep tray that will fit all the bread. Cut the crusts off the bread. Soak the bread in the milk mixture, turning the slices over a few times and spooning the mixture over the bread. Leave to soak for 1–2 hours.

2. When ready to cook, turn the oven on low, about 60°C (140°F), and place two plates inside to keep warm.

3. Melt the butter in a large lidded frying pan until foaming. Add the bread, then cover and cook for 3 minutes. Turn the slices over and layer two of the slices with cheese and ham. Cover and cook for a further 3 minutes, or until the cheese has melted.

4. Sandwich the slices together, pressing lightly, and place on the warmed plates. For a sweet and salty breakfast, enjoy with maple syrup, if desired.

Coppe pan

コッペパン

90 ml (3 fl oz) water
40 ml (1¼ fl oz) milk
3 g (1 teaspoon) instant yeast
200 g (7 oz) bread flour
3 teaspoons sugar
½ teaspoon salt
15 g (½ oz) butter

These light bread rolls are the base for many konbini snacks, such as the napolitan bun, yakisoba bun, and buns filled with red bean paste and butter. They are also great for stuffing with your favourite salads and cold cuts, and as a hot dog bun.

Many children's bento wouldn't be complete without this little fluffy bun, which holds up so well to many different fillings.

1. In a microwave-safe bowl, mix together the water and milk. Microwave for 30 seconds, or until the liquid is body temperature. Add the yeast, then cover and leave for 5 minutes, or until frothy.

2. In the bowl of a stand mixer, combine the flour, sugar and salt. Pour in the milk mixture and mix on low speed for 5 minutes. Add the butter and knead for another 5–10 minutes, until you have a dough that is smooth and elastic.

3. Cover the dough and leave to rise in a warm place for 1 hour, or until doubled in size.

4. Divide the dough into eight even pieces and shape into rounds. Cover and rest for another 10 minutes.

5. Roll each ball out into a 10 x 18 cm (4 x 7 inch) rectangle. Fold in the long sides, overlapping them. Pinch the seams closed, press in the ends, then flip them over onto a baking tray, or into coppe pan moulds if you have them. Cover and allow to rise for a final 20–30 minutes, until doubled in size.

6. Meanwhile preheat the oven to 190° C (375° F).

7. Place the buns in the oven, then carefully pour about 125 ml (½ cup) of water into a heatproof bowl and place it in the bottom of the oven to create steam. Bake for 12 minutes or until the buns are golden brown and make a hollow noise when tapped.

8. Remove the buns from the oven and allow to cool completely before using. If not eating the same day, store in an airtight bag at room temperature and they'll stay fresh for up to 3 days.

VARIATION

Mochipan

もちパン

These chewy little bread rolls with a mochi texture can be used as a stand-in for a bagel. Fill with smoked salmon, cream cheese and capers for a pleasant midday snack. Follow the coppe pan recipe above, but replace 30 g (1 oz) of the bread flour with 30 g (1 oz) of tapioca starch and shape into rounds.

Filling suggestions

Napolitan pasta (page 138)
Yakisoba (page 146)
Tamago (page 39)
Karaage (page 76) and cheese
Red bean paste and butter

Uzumaki pan

渦巻きパン

Filling
10 g (⅓ oz) bread flour
6 g (¼ oz) cocoa powder
60 ml (¼ cup) milk
30 g (1 oz) sugar
1 egg
60 g (2 oz) chocolate,
    roughly chopped
1 x quantity rested Coppe pan
    (see opposite)

Egg wash
1 tablespoon milk
½ egg (reserved from
    the filling above)

Uzumaki pan, or spiral-shaped bread, uses the same base as the coppe pan opposite, but is filled and shaped into a spiral, so there's filling in every bite. This recipe is for a chocolate version, but you can replace the chocolate filling with sweet potato, pumpkin or taro paste, or even cheese and corn.

1. To make the filling, put the flour, cocoa powder, milk and sugar in a microwave-safe bowl. Beat the egg in a small jug and add half to the flour mixture, reserving the remainder for the egg wash. Whisk thoroughly, then microwave in 30-second bursts for 1–1½ minutes, until the mixture is thick, like a dough. While the mixture is still hot, add the chocolate, mixing to combine and melt the chocolate.

2. Tip the filling out onto a sheet of plastic wrap and press out into a 13 cm (5 inch) square.

3. Roll the rested coppe pan out into a 20 cm (8 inch) square. Place the chocolate filling in the centre, then spread the filling into a diamond shape, with the points extending to the midway point of each straight edge of dough. Bring the four corners of dough together to encase the chocolate.

4. Using a rolling pin, roll the dough out into a rectangle, about 40 cm (16 inches) wide and 25 cm (10 inches) long. Fold the short sides into the centre, then roll out again into a 20 x 30 cm (8 x 12 inch) rectangle.

5. Cut the dough lengthways into six pieces. Take each piece and twist it, then twirl it into a bun, securing the ends underneath. Place on a baking tray lined with baking paper, leaving a 10 cm (4 inch) gap between each bun. Cover and leave to rest for 1 hour.

6. Preheat the oven to 180° C (350° F).

7. Mix the milk with the reserved beaten egg from the filling to make an egg wash. Brush the buns with the egg wash, then bake for 15 minutes, or until the buns are golden brown and make a hollow noise when tapped.

Behind the Konbini:
A chat with Lawson

We sat down with Lawson's Mochimaru Ken-san to find out how konbinis keep coming up with novel products, and what keeps them ahead of the game.

Q **Japan's konbinis are famous for their high rotation of limited-edition products and collaborations. How do you keep coming up with these, and keep customer interest and loyalty high?**

A We use a point card system called Ponta [author's note: Ponta-kun is its kawaii mascot] that enables us to track purchase data in our stores, and this, combined with market research, helps us stay on top of our customers' needs and preferences. Due to the density of Lawson stores, we can track the preferences of customers within a 365-metre radius, and we know they are locals as they tend to walk instead of drive.

We also have a dedicated development team broken up across eight different areas in Japan, each one tasked with creating limited-edition items.

Our head office product development team taps into popular games or anime, seasonal holidays [for Halloween, Lawson launched an apple caramel dora-mochi, a pumpkin caramel tart and an apple caramel mousse cake], or ongoing collaborations with popular Japanese brands such as Godiva chocolate and Sarutahiko Coffee. We recently partnered with The Legend of Zelda to release a range of limited-edition original food and drinks – a dry curry onigiri, 'animal' meat curry-pan, 'max truffle' kinoko (mushroom) focaccia, a 'max salmon' and fresh milk cream chowder, and banana au lait.

Depending on the season, we might introduce variations on our premium roll cake and karaage. [In summer, there was sudachi Karaage-Kun, and his sea-loving friends, prawn (shrimp) and fish nuggets joined the fray; in autumn, the premium roll cake had been given a dark chocolate touch.]

Brand trust and loyalty are two things our customers value highly, so we also look to collaborations with trusted restaurants. For example, we partnered with renowned bakery/curry house, Shinjuku Nakamuraya (est. 1901) on a range of curry bento (katsu, Frankfurt, korokke and beef), and for the 2024 osechi ryori (New Year's jubako), we've partnered with renowned restaurant Sengaya and Hokkaido's seafood wholesaler Marusui.

We also came together with one of Uji's renowned tea shops, Morihan (est.1836) for a range of green tea sweets which included matcha and cream dora-mochi, matcha baum-keki (baumkuchen), matcha tsutsumi (matcha cream and matcha sauce encased in a mochi filling), matcha meron-pan, matcha an-pan and matcha kakigori. All of these are sold for a limited time only, and our development teams work on identifying new businesses to keep things fresh.

What sets us apart from supermarkets is our ability to introduce new products quickly. We release about 100 new products each week on Tuesdays, launched on Lawson's website. We are also known as the konbini with the healthy natural products [Natural Lawson, which started with the concept of 「美しく健康で快適な」 a 'beautiful, healthy and comfortable' lifestyle for women] and sustainability. Younger Japanese are becoming more environmentally conscious, which is why we've introduced the Green Lawson trial store, actively reducing packaging and setting a goal to reduce carbon dioxide and plastic. We're striving to realise a sustainable society, and develop products that consider the natural environment.

Q   **How do you decide on what products will make it into a konbini, and what to introduce?**

A   In the past, konbinis were seen as places to buy food and beverages such as onigiri, sando and bento in the morning and afternoon. This shifted during the pandemic. Customers changed their purchasing behaviour and tended to avoid supermarkets and restaurants, preferring instead to shop at their local konbini – since there is always one nearby.

The feedback we received was that it would be convenient to have an assortment of products necessary for daily life, such as tofu, milk and bread, at their familiar local Lawson store, and this marked our move towards selling more everyday items under our Lawson umbrella. [Japanese staples, such as regional soba, udon, rice, wakame, tinned grilled saury with kabayaki sauce, and cartons of houjicha, mugicha and sencha can now be found at Lawson stores.]

We've also seen a lifestyle change towards 'new convenience' – more frozen foods, daily food, fresh bento and sozai (side dishes). Since 2011, we've had Machikado kitchens in our stores, strengthened during the pandemic to include freshly cooked bento (instead of refrigerated ones), which are designed to be prepared by anyone – whether they are high school students or staff with limited cooking skills. Already these are proving more popular than our refrigerated bento.

For everyday products, we introduced MUJI to our stores in earnest in May 2022. In convenience stores so far, the demand for daily necessities has been centred on 'emergency purchasing', but we wanted to establish our stores as a new place to buy daily products through the MUJI brand. [As such, you'll find MUJI inner wear, socks, body towels, stationery, storage and even MUJI nail polish in Lawson stores].

We also partnered with Korean beauty brand 'Rom&nd' on a special range – '&nd by rom&nd' – in our stores, as Korean beauty is popular in Japan at the moment.

Recently, we have also introduced food and daily goods for solos and couples. This is a reflection of the living arrangements in society, where we are finding a lot more solo customers, whether young or elderly. Each Lawson store has a different layout, depending on what the owners feel best meets the interest of the customer. If it's near a school, that Lawson store will have Gachapon machines, more candy and little affordable snacks.

Q   **Can you tell us about the region-specific products?**

A   Our regional products are very popular, and given the preferences of different parts of Japan, responding to the different food cultures in each area is important. For example, we might stock products with a soy sauce base in Tokyo versus a soup stock base in Kansai – what we call our 'community-based x individual customers x individual store principle'.

Right now, being autumn, we are selling chūkaman (Chinese buns) where the fillings are shoyu (soy) or shio (salt) based, depending on the area. The east side of Japan prefers heavier flavours, so the chūkaman sold there have a familiar soy flavour. The west side of Japan, however, prefers lighter flavours, so we sell a shoyu and shio chūkaman there. For travellers – both Japanese and from overseas – this means that visiting a familiar Lawson store in another prefecture will yield them interesting regional products they can't find in their own hometown or city.

We also use our stores to launch products from different regions. We have a plain rice onigiri featuring rice from different rice-growing regions of Japan, to introduce the different rice types across the country. We have also recently launched a nation-wide bento featuring specialty bento from different areas. For Hokkaido, this is a pork chop bento with Sunagawa onion sauce. Tohoku has an Aizu katsu don, Northern Kanto has a sweet and spicy tare don, Tokyo has a barbecue bento, Chubu has a Taiwanese-style spicy don, Kinki has a B-Gurume (gourmet) 'Bokkake' soba meshi with sweet and spicy beef tendon and konjac, Chugoku has a sweet and spicy sliced fried chicken meshi, and Kyushu has a pork and leek 'stamina' don with leek from Ōita prefecture.

Q   **How much focus do you place on Japanese-made products, and do you actively seek out working with local farmers, artisans and producers?**

A   The local community places a great emphasis on Japan-made and Japan-produced products, and given the daily movement of goods in our stores, we have to be able to stably procure the raw materials required for our goods.

One of the initiatives we have undertaken is 'Lawson Farm' – an agricultural land-owned qualified corporation at 17 locations throughout Japan. Essentially, we have partnered with farms to provide locally grown vegetables and fruits to us. The farms use the 'Nakashima Farming method', which diagnoses the soil and nurtures it to create ideal conditions before the crops are planted. This produces delicious and healthy vegetables and fruits, and is also good for soil health.

6 Desserts

デザート

Banana boats 220

Black sugar steamed cakes 222

Choux cream puffs 224

Coffee jelly parfait 226

White taiyaki 237

Custard cream 237

Croissant taiyaki 237

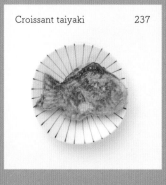

More than just an ice-cream freezer,* konbini serve incredible desserts.

Here you'll find the kissaten (coffee shop) classics, such as coffee jelly parfait and purin (crème caramel), tiramisu, matchamisu (matcha tiramisu), and desserts of the lightest cream paired with the fruit of the season – from strawberries to Shine Muscat grapes.

At Ministop, you'll even find limited-edition 'soft cream' (what soft serve is known as in Japan) and fruit parfaits – made at the store with soft cream, fresh fruit from famed local regions in limited-edition flavours, and fruit purée.

From a popular Shinkansen snack to puddings served at kissatens late into the night, our final chapter contains desserts that can be enjoyed any time of day, as they would if a sudden craving comes upon you when passing a konbini in Japan.

Daifuku   228
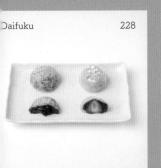

Dorayaki   230
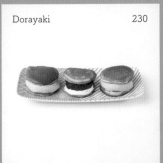

Purin   232

Yaki-purin   234

* Don't overlook the ice-cream freezers of konbinis either! These contain some of the best options: limited-edition, Japan-only seasonal flavours of Häagen-Dazs; ice-cream daifuku; and Hokkaido milk ice cream in the Hokkaido konbini chain, Seicomart.

Banana boats

バナナボート

1 small banana, 12–15 cm
  (4¾–6 inches) long, peeled
  and cut in half lengthways
1 teaspoon lemon juice
80 ml (⅓ cup) cream
1½ teaspoons sugar

Batter

2 eggs
2 tablespoons sugar
½ teaspoon neutral-flavoured oil
50 g (⅓ cup) flour

Rum sauce

20 ml (¾ fl oz) rum
1½ tablespoons sugar
20 ml (¾ fl oz) water

A simple handheld cake of bananas and sweet cream encased in a rum-scented pancake, this dessert is most often sold in konbinis near Shinkansen stations, as its portable form suits train travel perfectly. It's all the flavours of a cake in an easy-to-eat package, and one of our favourite things to take on board a long Shinkansen ride.

1. To make the batter, separate the egg whites and yolks. Using an electric mixer, whisk the egg whites to stiff peaks with the sugar. In a bowl, mix the egg yolks with the oil, then fold the beaten egg whites through. Sift in the flour and mix gently.

2. Cut two sheets of baking paper to fit the bottom of a small, lidded saucepan. Heat the saucepan over medium heat and place one of the baking paper sheets on the bottom. You may need a little oil to help it stick.

3. Pour in half the batter and spread it over the baking paper, to a diameter of about 15 cm (6 inches). Put the lid on, turn the heat to low and cook for 3 minutes. Once the pancake has puffed, place the second baking paper sheet on top and flip the pancake over. Cover with the lid and cook for a further 3 minutes.

4. Remove the pancake from the pan and repeat with the remaining batter. Allow to cool.

5. In a saucepan, heat all the rum sauce ingredients until the sugar has dissolved. Remove from the heat and set aside.

6. Brush the banana slices with the lemon juice. Whip the cream and sugar together into soft peaks.

7. Remove the baking paper from the cooled pancakes and brush them generously with the rum syrup. Spread the whipped cream over, leaving a 1.5 cm (½ inch) border around the edge. Place a banana slice in the centre of each pancake and fold the pancakes over, encasing them in cream. Wrap in plastic wrap and press the edges together.

8. Refrigerate to firm up the cream and eat within 24 hours.

Black sugar steamed cakes

Makes 9

黒糖蒸しパン

80 g (2¾ oz) brown sugar
    or Okinawa black sugar
60 ml (¼ cup) milk
pinch of salt
1½ tablespoons
    neutral-flavoured oil
1 egg
100 g (⅔ cup) cake flour
1 teaspoon baking powder

In the bakery aisle of konbinis, you'll find nestled amongst the roll cakes and coppe pan (fluffy buns) more traditional sweets such as odango, daifuku and, depending on the season, tsukimi keki (moon-viewing cakes) or sakura mochi. The black sugar steamed bun – or kurosato mushi pan – is one of them.

You'll find these bite-sized steamed cakes all around Japan, most often in small country towns, where vendors sell them on the street. You'll also find variations in onsen districts, which use the hot steam from the onsens to cook the buns.

The sugar used greatly affects the end product, so use a good-quality, flavourful sugar here, such as Okinawa black sugar or a nice brown sugar.

1. In a bowl, whisk together the sugar, milk and salt until the salt and sugar have dissolved. (If the sugar is difficult to dissolve, microwave the mixture in 10-second bursts, mixing after each cooking burst until the sugar has dissolved.) Whisk in the oil and egg. Sift in the flour and baking powder and whisk until homogenous. Cover and allow to rest for 10 minutes.

2. Meanwhile, bring a large pot of water to the boil, and have a large steamer basket ready.

3. Prepare some waxed patty pan cups or sturdy paper muffin cases. (The batter will be quite liquid, so if using paper cases, you may need to use two or three of them for each bun, stacking them inside each other to keep their shape.)

4. Fill the paper cases two-thirds full of the batter.

5. Put the paper cases in the steamer basket, set it over the pan of boiling water and steam for 10–14 minutes over medium heat, depending on the size of your pan. The cakes are done when a skewer inserted in the middle comes out clean.

6. Remove the cakes from the steamer and allow to cool for 1 minute. The cakes are best served immediately.

Choux cream puffs

シュークリーム

150 ml (5 fl oz) cream
1 quantity of custard cream
    (page 237)

Craquelin

40 g (1½ oz) butter,
    at room temperature
40 g (1½ oz) light brown sugar
40 g (1½ oz) cake flour
½ teaspoon salt
½ teaspoon ground cinnamon

Choux

50 ml (1¾ fl oz) milk
50 ml (1¾ fl oz) water
50 g (1¾ oz) butter
1 teaspoon salt
1 teaspoon sugar
50 g (⅓ cup) cake flour
2 eggs, at room temperature

These puffball-like desserts are a nostalgic delight, the crisp pastry exterior and sweet custard filling never getting old. In konbinis you'll find choux with all manner of different creams: matcha, coffee, chocolate, strawberry... There's always a choux cream with a flavour that changes seasonally, though vanilla is always a staple.

Change the taste and complexion by adding various flavours (matcha powder, instant coffee, freeze-dried crushed or fresh fruit) to the cream, or, like Kissa Hangetsu – a gorgeous modern kissaten in Kuramae, Tokyo – serve your cream puffs with lightly flavoured fruit cream and thin slices of fruit.

These puffs are topped with a craquelin, a sweet and crunchy cookie topping that makes them extra crunchy and buttery. You can skip this part if you don't have the time, or want a more classic choux cream puff.

1. To make the craquelin, place the butter and sugar in the bowl of a stand mixer fitted with a paddle attachment and beat until pale and fluffy. Add the flour, salt and cinnamon and beat until just combined. Sandwich the batter between two pieces of baking paper and roll out to a thickness of 2–3 mm (⅛ inch). Freeze until required.

2. For the choux, heat the milk, water, butter, salt and sugar in a saucepan over medium heat until the butter has melted. Add the flour and mix using a spatula until the dough comes away from the side of the pan.

3. Remove from the heat and continue mixing until just above body temperature (40°C/105°F). Slowly add the eggs, mixing in after each addition. When all the egg is incorporated, transfer the batter to a piping bag fitted with a round nozzle and set aside until cool.

4. Preheat the oven to 190°C (375°F).

5. Line a large baking tray with baking paper. Using a round cutter, draw nine 5 cm (2 inch) diameter circles on the baking paper, about 10 cm (4 inches) apart. Pipe the batter into the circles, to about 2.5–3 cm (1–1¼ inches) high.

6. Take the craquelin out of the freezer. Cut out 5 cm (2 inch) rounds and place them on the piped choux batter. Transfer to the oven and bake for 20 minutes.

7. Turn the heat down to 170°C (340°F). Rotate the baking tray and bake for a further 20 minutes. The choux pastry puffs are done when they sound hollow when tapped. Remove from the oven and allow to cool completely.

8. Whisk the cream to stiff peaks. In a separate bowl, whisk the custard to make it smooth. Using a spatula, slowly incorporate the whipped cream into the custard, being careful not to beat the air out of the cream. Transfer to a piping bag fitted with a round nozzle.

9. Using a small knife, make a hole in the cooled choux puffs, then pipe in the cream.

10. Chill for 1 hour to set the cream. Serve within 1 day.

Coffee jelly parfait

コーヒーゼリーパフェ

100 ml (3½ fl oz) cream
2 teaspoons sugar
½ teaspoon natural vanilla
    extract
4 tablespoons cornflakes
2 scoops of vanilla ice cream
2 mint sprigs

Coffee jelly
200 ml (7 fl oz) black coffee
1 tablespoon sugar, or to taste
1½ teaspoons gelatine powder

Jelly may be less popular now in the West than it was in the 1980s, but Japan has a long-held love for jelly that will never fade. There are many traditional sweets, or wagashi (和菓子), that are simple coloured jellies set with agar agar, a seaweed extract. You'll find these in konbinis, the most common being yokan, a shelf-stable jelly of red bean paste.

Our recipe is for coffee jelly, a dessert referenced in many manga and anime. You can use instant black coffee, or, if you're a coffee lover, your single-origin beans. Coffee jelly is a dessert that can be tweaked to any taste.

Here, we've turned the jelly into a parfait – as you'd find in a kissaten – with cornflakes adding crunch, and ice cream and cream lending richness and a cafe latte feel to the dessert.

1. To make the jelly, bring the coffee and sugar to a simmer in a small saucepan, stirring to dissolve the sugar. Take off the heat, add the gelatine and whisk until the gelatine has dissolved. Pour into a small baking tray to a depth of 1.5 cm (½ inch). Refrigerate for 2–3 hours to set the jelly.

2. When the jelly has set, cut into 1.5 cm (½ inch) cubes, or use a spoon to break it into smaller pieces. Refrigerate until needed.

3. When ready to serve, use an electric beater to whisk together the cream, sugar and vanilla extract to soft peaks.

4. Set out two serving glasses. In each, place 2 tablespoons of cornflakes, then 2 tablespoons of whipped cream, and a layer of coffee jelly, finishing with a scoop of ice cream. Garnish with the mint sprigs and serve.

Daifuku

大福

Known outside Japan as mochi, daifuku are small rounds of mochi stuffed with a sweet filling – traditionally red or white bean paste, but extending to fruit and ice cream in more recent times.

The following recipes keep the fillings traditional, but alter the mochi layer for different flavours.

If you don't like red bean paste (you'll have a difficult time in Japan!), swap out the red bean for any filling you like, or add fruit to the filling. Strawberries are a perennial favourite.

Soy milk daifuku

豆乳大福

Makes 8

200 g (7 oz) red bean paste
4 tablespoons potato starch

Soy mochi
200 ml (7 fl oz) soy milk
120 g (4 oz) shiratamako or
    glutinous rice flour
30 g (1 oz) sugar

1. Divide the red bean paste into eight even pieces and roll into balls.

2. To make the mochi, microwave the soy milk in a microwave-safe bowl for 1–2 minutes, until hot. Mix the shiratamako and sugar in a microwave-safe bowl. Add the soy milk a little at a time, whisking constantly until a smooth batter is formed. Cover with plastic wrap and microwave for 2 minutes at 500 watts. Mix with a spatula, then microwave for another 1 minute.

3. Sprinkle the potato starch on a clean bench Divide the mochi mixture into eight equal portions. Using the potato starch to prevent sticking, roll each portion out to 1 cm (½ inch) thick. Fill each portion with a piece of red bean paste and wrap the mochi around.

4. Place seam side down on a serving plate. For the best texture, enjoy on the day of making.

Black sesame daifuku

黒胡麻大福

Makes 8

30 g (1 oz) black sesame paste
170 g (6 oz) red bean paste
4 tablespoons potato starch
4 tablespoons kinako (roasted soy bean flour)

Black sesame mochi
120 g (4½ oz) shiratamako or
    glutinous rice flour
30 g (1 oz) sugar
180 ml (6 fl oz) hot water
30 g (1 oz) black sesame paste

1. Mix together the black sesame paste and red bean paste. Divide into eight even pieces and roll into balls.

2. To make the mochi, mix the shiratamako and sugar in a microwave-safe bowl. Slowly whisk in the water, then the black sesame paste, until the mixture is homogenous and no lumps are seen. Wrap and microwave for 2 minutes at 500 watts. Mix with a spatula, then microwave for another 1 minute.

3. Sprinkle the potato starch on a clean bench. Divide the mochi mixture into eight equal portions. Using the potato starch to prevent sticking, roll each portion out to 1 cm (½ inch) thick. Fill each portion with a piece of the red bean and sesame paste and wrap the mochi around.

4. Place seam side down on a serving plate and dust liberally with the kinako. For the best texture, enjoy on the day of making.

Note
If using strawberries for the soy milk daifuku, remove the green hulls, and use 35 g (1¼ oz) of red bean paste for each daifuku. Place the red bean paste on a piece of plastic wrap, flatten with your palm, place the strawberry in the centre, then wrap with the red bean paste. Place on a tray and repeat with the remaining strawberries. (You can reuse the same plastic wrap for all strawberries.) Wrap in mochi as above.

Dorayaki

どら焼き

2 large eggs
1 tablespoon honey
1 tablespoon water
½ teaspoon vegetable oil
65 g (2¼ oz) granulated sugar
85 g (3 oz) cake flour
½ teaspoon bicarbonate of soda
    (baking soda)
1 tablespoon neutral-flavoured
    oil, for greasing
red bean paste, for filling

Named after a small gong, dorayaki are said to have been invented almost a thousand years ago when a samurai named Benkei left his gong at a farmer's house, and the farmer used the gong to make small, round pancakes. We'll never know whether that story is true, but what is true is that the Japanese love dorayaki, and there is rarely an area in the country where you won't find these round sweets.

Dorayaki are a konbini staple, and on National Dorayaki Day (4 April), you'll find special attention given to this traditional treat. Once (and still) filled with red bean and cream, these days you'll also find dorayaki with fresh fruit, custard, matcha, ice cream, chocolate and chestnut cream fillings.

They are great with a cup of hot tea to end a meal, and can be made in advance and wrapped tightly to stop them drying out. Our recipe below is for the dorayaki themselves, which you can then fill to your liking.

1. Crack the eggs into a large bowl. Add the honey, water, vegetable oil and sugar and whisk together until the sugar has dissolved. Sift in the flour and bicarbonate of soda and whisk until combined. Cover with plastic wrap and allow to rest for 20 minutes.

2. Heat a large non-stick frying pan over medium heat. Wipe the pan with a thin layer of oil.

3. Using about 1½ tablespoons per pancake, add the batter to the pan, keeping a gap between each pancake as they will expand during cooking. Turn the heat to low and cook the pancakes for 2 minutes or until golden brown underneath. Flip over and cook for 1 minute more. Remove from the pan and allow to cool.

4. To serve, simply spread some red bean paste over half the pancakes, to your taste, then sandwich the other pancakes on top for a classic dorayaki. The dorayaki are best enjoyed the day they are made.

Purin

プリン

90 g (3 oz) sugar
250 ml (1 cup) milk
100 ml (3½ fl oz) cream
3 eggs
1 teaspoon pure vanilla paste
    or natural vanilla extract

Caramel
100 g (3½ oz) sugar
40 ml (1¼ fl oz) water

This delicate, silky, vanilla-spiked custard is a wonderful little treat to end
a meal, with the sweetness of the custard balanced by the slight bitterness
from the caramel sauce. We can't go past one in a konbini, kissaten (one of
our favourites being the one at Kayaba, whose purin are topped with candied
nuts), or the ones sold in regional areas (Nara, Shiroishi-Zao), flavoured with
sake, matcha or coffee, or topped with tiny jewelled cubes of local fruit.

In Japan, each region showcases their very best dairy or eggs in their purin;
the quality of these ingredients really shines through given the simple nature
of the dish. A Hokkaido purin might highlight the fantastic dairy of the region,
while nearby Akita will showcase the famous Jidori chicken eggs, their purin
taking on a bright orange hue from the rich yolks.

This recipe sets the dessert in small glass jars, as they do in Japan,
but you can use ramekins too. Just divide the mixture among 4–6 ramekins,
and increase the baking time. The purin are done when a knife inserted into
the centre comes out clean.

1. Preheat the oven to 150°C (300°F).

2. Place the sugar in a large mixing
   bowl. Bring the milk to a simmer
   in a small saucepan, then pour
   over the sugar. Whisk until the
   sugar has dissolved, then add the
   cream, eggs and vanilla, whisking
   to incorporate. Strain through a
   fine-meshed sieve and chill for
   30 minutes to 1 hour, until the
   custard comes back down to
   room temperature.

3. Make a dry caramel by placing the
   sugar in a clean small saucepan
   over medium heat. Cook, swirling
   regularly, until a caramel is achieved.
   Remove from the heat. Add the
   water, taking care as the caramel
   will splutter, and stir until combined.
   Divide the mixture among nine small
   heatproof glass jars, about 65 ml
   (2¼ fl oz) in capacity.

4. Pour in the cooled custard mixture,
   cover each jar tightly with foil and
   place in a deep baking dish. Bring
   a pot or kettle of water to the boil,
   then carefully pour the boiling
   water into the baking dish, halfway
   up the jars.

5. Carefully transfer the dish to the
   oven and cook the custards for
   15–18 minutes, until set.

6. Remove from the oven, discard
   the water and chill the custards
   for about 2 hours, until cold.
   The custards will keep, covered
   in the fridge, for up to 3 days.

Yaki-purin

焼きプリン

115 g (4 oz) sugar
250 ml (1 cup) milk
300 ml (10 fl oz) cream
3 eggs
1 tablespoon pure vanilla paste

Caramel
100 g (3½ oz) sugar
40 ml (1¼ fl oz) water

Yaki-purin is a cross between a crème caramel and a baked custard. The surface develops a beautiful golden-brown, caramelised texture, and while this can be eaten chilled, we enjoy it warm, straight out of the oven.

For purin-lovers, it is the cold-weather alternative to the chilled purin dessert on the previous pages.

1. Preheat the oven to 180°C (350°F).

2. Make a dry caramel by placing the sugar in a clean small saucepan over medium heat. Cook, swirling regularly, until a caramel is achieved. Remove from the heat. Add the water, taking care as the caramel will splutter, and stir until combined. Divide among four 250 ml (1 cup) ramekins.

3. Place the sugar in a large mixing bowl. Bring 100 ml (3½ fl oz) of the milk to a simmer in a small saucepan, then pour over the sugar. Whisk until the sugar has dissolved, then add the remaining milk, the cream, eggs and vanilla, whisking to incorporate. Strain through a fine-meshed sieve.

4. Pour the mixture into the ramekins and place them in a deep baking dish.

5. Bring a pot or kettle of water to the boil, then carefully pour the boiling water into the baking dish, halfway up the ramekins.

6. Carefully transfer to the oven and bake for 40 minutes, or until set.

7. Carefully remove from the oven and allow to cool for 10 minutes before serving. The custards can also be served chilled, and will keep, covered in the fridge, for up to 3 days.

Taiyaki

鯛焼き

neutral-flavoured oil,
    for greasing
200 ml (7 fl oz) milk
50 g (1¾ oz) shiratamako or
    glutinous rice flour
2 tablespoons sugar
1 egg
1 teaspoon honey
1 tablespoon taihaku oil
    (see note) or neutral-
    flavoured oil
150 g (1 cup) cake flour
2 teaspoons baking powder
6 tablespoons filling
    (see options below)

A traditional Japanese sweet in the shape of a lucky tai (鯛), or sea bream, taiyaki is best described as a sweet, filled waffle. Red bean paste is the classic filling, with custard close behind. More recently, savoury taiyaki have made an appearance, with ham and cheese being the most popular.

    The exterior of the taiyaki is just as important as the filling, and this is where the taiyaki has become more interesting. For more crunch and butteriness, you can now find puff pastry replacing the waffle mix, creating a croissant taiyaki. There's also white taiyaki, which blends different tapioca flours for a pure-white taiyaki with a chewy, mochi-like bite.

Note

Taihaku oil is a white sesame oil with a very mild flavour, and can be found in Asian and Japanese grocery stores.

Suggested fillings

Red bean paste
Ham and cheese
Custard cream (see opposite)

1. Heat a taiyaki waffle iron over medium–low heat and grease well with neutral-flavoured oil.

2. Microwave the milk for 1–2 minutes, until hot. Combine the shiratamako and sugar in a small bowl. Slowly pour in the milk, stirring to dissolve the sugar and to make a smooth paste.

3. Add the egg, honey and taihaku oil. Whisk well to combine. Sift in the flour and baking powder. Whisk gently until just combined.

4. Spoon 1–2 tablespoons of the batter into the waffle iron, spread it out using a spatula and place a tablespoon of your chosen filling in the centre. Add more batter to cover well and close the waffle iron. Turn the heat down low and cook for about 5 minutes, turning over halfway. The taiyaki is done when it is golden brown on both sides and comes away easily from the waffle iron.

5. Remove the taiyaki from the iron, clean the iron with paper towel, oil again and repeat with the remaining batter and filling. Serve when cooled slightly, as the inside will be very hot.

White taiyaki

白い鯛焼き

Makes about 6, depending on your waffle iron size

100 g (⅔ cup) cake flour
50 g (1¾ oz) tapioca starch
2 teaspoons sugar
1½ tablespoons skim milk powder
½ teaspoon baking powder
½ teaspoon salt
1 egg white
150 ml (5 fl oz) water
6 tablespoons filling (see options opposite)

1. In a bowl, mix together the flour, tapioca starch, sugar, milk powder, baking powder and salt. In a separate bowl, whisk the egg white and water.

2. Pour the dry ingredients into the wet ingredients, whisking to create a cream-like consistency. If the batter is too firm, add more water, a tablespoon at a time, to achieve the correct viscosity.

3. Follow the instructions opposite to cook the taiyaki.

Custard cream

カスタードクリーム

Makes enough for about 6 taiyaki

For a dark chocolate custard, use dark chocolate instead of white chocolate. For a coffee-flavoured cream, add some instant coffee powder to the custard as it's being cooked.

120 ml (4 fl oz) milk
50 ml (1¾ fl oz) cream
3 egg yolks
1½ tablespoons sugar
1½ tablespoons cornflour (cornstarch)
1 teaspoon nautural vanilla extract
40 g (1½ oz) white chocolate

Place all the ingredients except the chocolate in a stainless steel saucepan. Heat gently, whisking until thickened, being careful not to overcook, otherwise the eggs will scramble. The mixture should reach about 80°C (175°F). Remove from the heat, add the chocolate and whisk until melted. Pass through a fine-meshed sieve to remove any lumps, then place in a container with plastic wrap on the surface to prevent a skin forming. Chill until cold.

Croissant taiyaki

クロワッサン鯛焼き

Makes 2

neutral-flavoured oil, for greasing
1 frozen puff pastry sheet, thawed, cut in half
1 tablespoon sugar
2–3 tablespoons filling (see options opposite)

1. Heat a taiyaki waffle iron over medium–low heat and grease well with neutral-flavoured oil.

2. Cut each half of the puff pastry sheet to fit your waffle iron. Make one sheet for the bottom and the top. Lightly sprinkle the pastry on both sides with sugar.

3. Place one pastry sheet on the waffle iron. Add 1–1½ tablespoons of your chosen filling, then cover with the second pastry sheet and close the waffle iron.

4. Cook for about 4 minutes, then turn over and cook for another 4 minutes. After that time, check the colour of the pastry by opening the waffle iron. It should be golden brown all over. If not, continue cooking.

5. When uniformly browned, remove from the waffle iron. Using scissors, cut off any burnt or excess pastry. Allow to rest for 4–5 minutes, then serve.

Final Reflections

JAPAN HAS ALWAYS MAINTAINED A delicate balance between tradition and modernity, and there is little doubt the konbini represents everything modern that Japan is known for. Efficiency, convenience, fluorescent lights, a dazzling range of different products beautifully presented within a compact space... and questionable amounts of packaging. Thankfully, steps are being taken to combat this latter problem. Notably, the once ubiquitous disposable cutlery – wrapped in more packaging – is now available only on request. In most Japanese stores, you'll now be asked if you'd like to purchase a bag, and more Japanese are carrying canvas tote bags to place their shopping in.

Away from the markets, sleepy shōtengai – the vegetable and fruit growers purveying their produce in bamboo baskets – and the standalone shops where staff smartly attired in pressed white coats and peaked hats sell their wares, the konbini is a place where you can find almost everything. For some it is a daily or nightly ritual – taking home lunch, dinner, snacks, dessert, medicine, beer and entertainment.

Still, we felt conflicted. Is the konbini truly a shakai infura (social infrastructure) – and what is the cost of this convenience? But travelling to rural Japan, then meeting with Lawson and hearing their stories – and the passion and genuine-ness with which these stories were relayed – imprinted one thing upon us. They weren't hiding behind the shiny veneer of a corporation, though profits would naturally factor into the business, and some decisions would be motivated by supply-chain control and monetary reasons. They truly, genuinely, saw themselves as part of society, and the betterment of society.

Whether during the 3/11 earthquake, the pandemic or in Japan's rural reaches, the konbinis saw themselves as servicing the people. And in places Japanese society had forgotten, where shops had long shuttered and towns were slowly becoming derelict, we could see how critical having a familiar konbini – a hub with all the services and daily necessities – could be.

Rather than a replacement for all that has been lost, konbinis are, rather, places that keep communities running. A way to provide a service to the citizens, and among the modernness, offer the bite-sized comfort of small traditions: mitarashi dango, daifuku, dorayaki and onigiri.

Basics, glossary & index

基本 レシピ

Onsen eggs

温泉卵

Makes 2

These eggs are traditionally cooked in hot springs, or onsens, from which they derive their name. In the 60°C (140°F) hot springs, the egg whites set into a jelly-like state, while the yolks remain runny, despite being cooked. They are used to top donburi, or rice dishes, are added to noodle soups for richness and body, or used as a dipping sauce for tsukune.

Here is a quick and easy way to cook eggs, with the result very similar to onsen eggs – but without the precise temperature control or timing required for traditional onsen eggs.

1 litre (4 cups) water
2 eggs

1. In a saucepan, bring the water to the boil, then turn off the heat. When the bubbles slow down, carefully use a slotted spoon to slide the whole eggs into the water. Leave in the water for 11 minutes.

2. Remove the eggs and place in a bowl. Run cold water over the eggs for 1 minute, or until the eggs are no longer hot.

3. Use immediately, or store in the refrigerator for up to 2 days.

Salad chicken

サラダチキン

Serves 2–4

A staple of convenience stores, and popular among busy office workers, a simple, well-cooked chicken breast can be used for a variety of purposes. The name derives from the fact that the chicken is usually used in salads and cold preparations.

2 boneless chicken breasts, about 250 g (9 oz) each, skin on or off
2 tablespoons neutral-flavoured oil
2 teaspoons salt
½ teaspoon black pepper
6 slices of fresh ginger
2 spring onions (scallions), green part only, cut into 3 cm (1¼ inch) lengths
2 litres (8 cups) water

1. Place each chicken breast in an individual heatproof snap-lock bag, then add half the oil, salt and pepper to each and massage briefly. Divide the ginger and spring onion between the bags, placing them on the underside of each breast, not the smooth side. Seal the bags securely, expelling as much air as possible.

2. Pour the water into a large pot with a lid. Turn the heat up to high. While the water heats up, leave the sealed bags containing the chicken on the kitchen counter to come to room temperature.

3. If you have a cooking thermometer, bring the water to 80°C (175°F). Add the chicken, still in their bags; the chicken will lower the water temperature to around 70°C (160°F). Place the lid on and maintain the temperature of the water between 60°C and 70°C (140°F and 160°F) for 40 minutes, before removing the bags from the pot.

4. If you don't have a thermometer, bring the water to the boil, add the chicken, then turn off the heat and place a lid on. Leave for 40 minutes, then remove the chicken.

5. Once you have removed the chicken from the water, cool quickly by placing the bags in an ice bath or in cold water. Transfer to the refrigerator and use within 3 days.

Dashi

出汁

Makes about 1.5 litres (6 cups)

Makes about 750 ml (3 cups)

Method 1: The traditional way
2 litres (8 cups) filtered water, at room temperature
12 g (⅓ oz) kombu
25 g (1 oz) katsuobushi (bonito flakes)

1. Pour the water into a large pot. Add the kombu, then leave to steep for 30 minutes. Place the pot over high heat and, when bubbles start rising – when the water reaches about 70° C (160° F) – remove and reserve the kombu.

2. Bring the water temperature to about 80° C (175° F), then add the katsuobushi. Keep the heat on until it reaches 85° C (185° F), or small bubbles are rising, then turn off the heat.

3. When the katsuobushi sinks to the bottom of the pot, strain the dashi through a fine-meshed sieve or muslin (cheesecloth). Do not press on the katsuobushi as it will introduce unwanted flavours.

4. You can use the left-over katsuobushi and kombu to make niban dashi – 'second dashi' – by re-simmering the ingredients for 10 minutes, to make a good base for a stew.

5. Allow the dashi to cool, then refrigerate and use within 3 days.

Method 2: The quick way
750 ml (3 cups) water
1 instant dashi tea bag

1. Bring the water to a simmer in a small saucepan, then add the dashi tea bag. Press the tea bag down into the water and simmer for 1 minute.

2. Switch the heat off and taste the broth. If it's not strong enough, you can leave the dashi bag in for another 1–5 minutes.

3. When the broth is flavourful, remove the dashi bag and allow the liquid to cool if not using immediately.

Makes about 750 ml (3 cups)

Method 3: The instant way
750 ml (3 cups) boiling water
1 tablespoon hon dashi powder

Whisk together the boiling water and hon dashi powder. Taste and add more water or powder until you have a balanced dashi.

Glossary

Benishoga (紅生姜) is a variation of pickled ginger that's bright pink and cut into thin shards. The pink colour traditionally comes from umeboshi pickling liquid, but in more recent times comes from food colouring.

Bitter melon or goya (ゴーヤ) is an interesting-looking vegetable. Green with bumpy skin, like a bumpy cucumber, it almost doesn't look edible. It is bitter, but getting rid of the seeds and salting does alleviate some of the bitterness. If you like coffee or dark chocolate, you'll most likely enjoy the bitterness from this.

Black sugar or kurozato (黒砂糖) is an unrefined, black sugar that comes from the islands in the south of Japan. It is usually sold in large crystals and has a molasses-like taste. It is mainly used in traditional Japanese sweets and desserts.

Black vinegar (黒酢) is a fermented vinegar with a dark, soy sauce–like colour and a rich, complex flavour. It's great as a dipping sauce for pork dumplings and as an ingredient in dishes, as the acidity is well rounded but not overwhelming. You can find Chinese and Japanese varieties, each with their own characteristics. Both can be used in this book.

Chicken stock powder (鳥だしの素 or 鶏ガラスープ) is the distinctive flavour in many Chinese–Japanese dishes and adds a concentrated burst of umami. You can omit it, but some of the dish's characteristics will be lost. Chicken stock powder can be substituted with hon dashi powder.

Daikon (大根) is a long, white Japanese radish. It's very versatile and can be used raw, pickled or braised. Raw grated or shredded daikon is a very common palate cleanser in izakayas, and is known as daikon oroshi. With a dash of ponzu, daikon oroshi is a great side for grilled dishes.

Demi-glaze (デミグラス) is a reduced beef or veal stock popular in yōshoku (洋食) – Western dishes adapted to Japanese tastes. You can make your own by slowly reducing beef or veal stock to about a quarter of its original volume. If using store-bought stock to make demi-glaze, use a salt-reduced one, as a regular stock will end up extremely salty.

Kanimiso (蟹味噌) is the guts of a crab. It doesn't sound very appealing, but it has a wonderful, rich crab flavour. If you pick your own crab, you can find it in the shell (it's the brown part inside the head), or you can find it tinned in the frozen section of Asian grocery stores.

Kombu (昆布) are dried sheets of kelp with a strong savoury flavour, and a main ingredient in dashi. It can also be used to cure raw fish and seafood, by sandwiching the ingredient between two sheets of kombu, then leaving it to marinate for anywhere between 10 minutes for thin fish slices, and up to 1 day for whole fish fillets.

Mayonnaise (マヨ) used in this book is Japanese mayo. It is eggier than Western mayonnaise and has the addition of MSG to give it a distinctive flavour. Most Japanese brands have a similar flavour profile, based on a popular Japanese brand called Kewpie.

Mentaiko (明太子) is the salted, preserved roe of the Alaskan pollock fish, which is a type of cod. It has a clean, briny fish flavour with the added kick of chilli. Outside of Japan, it is usually sold frozen. Tarako (鱈子) is the non-spicy version.

Mirin (みりん) is type of rice wine made from glutinous rice that adds sweetness and umami to dishes. Real mirin or hon mirin should contain no added sugar, with the sweetness coming from the natural fermentation of glutinous rice with kōji (*Aspergillus oryzae*). Real mirin is expensive and difficult to find. Most store-bought mirin is a blend of real mirin (本みりん) and glucose syrup, and is fine to use in these recipes.

Miso paste (味噌) is a fermented paste containing soy beans and rice kōji (rice inoculated with spores to aid fermentation). Light-coloured miso pastes such as shiro miso, saikyo miso and mugi miso have a sweeter, lighter flavour, whereas dark misos like aka miso and hatcho miso are fermented longer and have a richer, almost soy sauce–like flavour. They are also generally saltier.

Natto (納豆) are fermented soy beans with a unique sticky texture, which is unfamiliar to many Western palates. It is an extremely nutritious topping for rice.

Nori (のり/海苔) are dried seaweed sheets commonly used to wrap sushi and onigiri. Good-quality nori is crisp, not chewy, and holds its structure well, as opposed to falling apart. It's delicious as a topping for ramen as it soaks up the ramen broth wonderfully, and is a great snack on its own. Most supermarkets now stock seaweed sheets; if not, check the snack aisle. These snack seaweeds can be used as toppings, but are usually quite salty, so be careful. They are also often small, which prevents them being used for sushi.

Panko (パン粉) are Japanese breadcrumbs that come in large shards, resulting in a shatteringly crisp crust on fried products. The dried version is found in most supermarkets these days. Fresh panko can be hard to find, but is sometimes in the frozen section of Asian supermarkets. Fresh panko has larger shards that work well with firm ingredients like pork steaks (as in tonkatsu) or hamburg steaks. Finer breadcrumbs work well with soft fillings such as béchamel croquettes.

Potato starch (片栗粉) is used in a variety of applications, from thickening soups and sauces to giving fried food a very crisp coating.

Rice (米) – every grain of rice is valuable, a lesson taught to every Japanese person from a very young age. There are many different types of Japanese rice, with varying grades of stickiness depending on whether it's table rice or sushi rice. Ask your grocery store about which rice is best for your purpose; rice from Niigata, Aomori, Akita or Hokkaido are good options. For making the sushi and onigiri recipes in chapter 1, look for koshihikari (コシヒカリ) rice. It has a nice short grain and pleasant stickiness that makes it easier to press together for onigiri and makizushi.

Rice vinegar (酢 or 米酢) has a mild tartness and sweetness that works for any Japanese salad dressing and as a vinegar base for pickling. It is much less astringent than Western vinegar, so substitute with caution.

Roasted sesame seed oil (ごま油) adds a pleasant nutty character to many dishes. It comes in a variety of grades, from cheap to expensive. The inexpensive versions are fine, but the higher-quality ones will add an extra dimension to your cooking.

Roasted sesame seeds (胡麻) are used either whole or crushed, and are a great way to add texture to sashimi, rice and salads. They can also come in a variety of flavours such as ume (pickled plum) or wasabi.

Sake (酒 or 料理酒) is in fact a general term for all alcohol – wine and spirits included. In this book we use it to refer to cooking sake. Sake is alcohol made from rice and kōji, and can add a floral and light flavour to dishes. For cooking, only use cooking sake or ryorishu. It has a simple, rounded flavour that pairs well with all food. Drinking sake can sometimes have unique flavours and characteristics that may not work well in cooking.

Shiratamako (白玉粉) is a glutinous rice flour used for making mochi and other Japanese desserts. You'll often find it comes in large pieces, so it's worthwhile blending it to make it easier to incorporate into doughs. Otherwise, mix it in the recipes with warm liquid to dissolve.

Shiso (しそ), also known as perilla leaf, comes in two varieties: a green variety called aojiso, and a purple variety called akajiso. The leaves have a distinct, herbaceous flavour, as do the delicate, tiny purple flowers (穂紫蘇), which are typically eaten with sashimi. Shiso can be found fresh in Asian greengrocers in the refrigerated section.

Soy sauce that we reference in recipes is koikuchi shoyu (濃口醤油) or dark soy sauce. It has a pleasant soy flavour and is moderately salty. We use a low-sodium variety (減塩). Please use this if you can find it. It allows you to adjust the soy flavour and salt to your liking.

Tamari (たまり醤油) is a dark soy sauce with a rich umami and caramel flavour. It works well with richer dishes such as braises, as it can overwhelm lighter dishes such as fish.

Tarako (鱈子) – see mentaiko.

Tobanjan (豆板醤), also known as doubanjiang, is a chilli sauce made from broad beans (fava beans). Most famously the flavouring for mapo tofu, it has a salty, savoury, spicy flavour that is the basis for many Korean, Sichuan and Japanese–Chinese dishes.

Umeboshi (梅干し) – pickled Japanese plums or apricots – can add a wonderful fruity sweetness and acidity to dishes. The colour and flavour come from pickling the fruit with red shiso leaves. Umeboshi is great mashed into a salad dressing or as a salty, sour accent to many dishes. Umeboshi is also commonly eaten on its own in the centre of a bowl of rice as a simple meal.

Usukuchi shoyu (薄口醤油) or light soy is lighter in colour than regular soy sauce, but don't let that deceive you. It's actually a little saltier – though it does have a lighter soy flavour. Use it when you want a milder soy taste or to keep a lighter colour in sauces and soups.

Yamaimo (山芋) or mountain potato is a sticky root vegetable that adds a unique (and sometimes polarising) texture to dishes. The texture can be described as somewhat slimy. Cooked chopped okra is a good substitute.

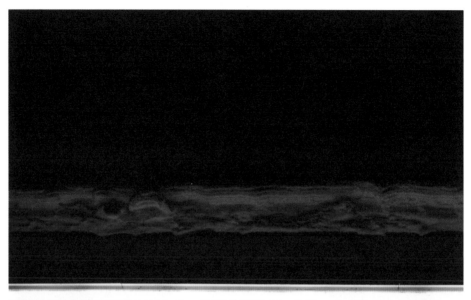

Index

7-Eleven _____ 9, 19, 33, 45, 57, 70

A

aburaage SEE tofu
amazu _____ 126
aonori
   Mentai okonomiyaki _____ 142
   Okonomiyaki toast _____ 206
   Omu-yakisoba _____ 146
   Roll pizza _____ 82
asparagus: Lemon cream pasta _____ 140
avocados
   Makizushi _____ 34–7
   Wanpaku sando _____ 190
Awase miso onigiri _____ 29

B

bacon
   Nikuman _____ 50
   Omu-yakisoba _____ 146
   Pizza toast _____ 204
   Pizzaman _____ 52
Banana boats _____ 220
batter _____ 176, 220
beans **246**
   Black sesame daifuku _____ 229
   Croissant taiyaki _____ 237
   Dorayaki _____ 230
   Gomaanman _____ 54
   Makizushi _____ 34–7
   Soy milk daifuku _____ 229
   Taiyaki _____ 236
   White taiyaki _____ 237
   SEE ALSO tobanjan
beef
   broth _____ 144
   Hamburg steaks _____ 100
   Hashed beef _____ 104
   Kalbi-don _____ 108
   Karē pan (Curry buns) _____ 114
   Keema curry _____ 112
   Meatballs _____ 102
   menchi katsu _____ 100
   Morioka reimen _____ 144
   Potato & beef croquettes _____ 61
   Rice buns with shigureni _____ 80
   shigureni (beef with ginger) _____ 80
bell peppers SEE capsicums
benishoga SEE ginger
bitter melon **246**
   Goya chanpuru _____ 121
Black sesame daifuku _____ 229
black sesame mochi _____ 229
Black sugar steamed cakes _____ 222
Black vinegar braised pork belly _____ 86
Blanched greens with miso
   sesame dressing _____ 124
bonito flakes SEE katsuobushi
brand collaborations _____ 107, 215–6

bread **165**
   Coppe pan _____ 210
   mochipan _____ 210
   Shokupan _____ 184
   Uzumaki pan _____ 211
brine _____ 156
broccolini: Lemon cream pasta _____ 140
broth _____ 144
buns
   Chūkaman _____ 46
   Gomaanman _____ 54
   Karēpan (Curry buns) _____ 114
   Maritozzo _____ 178
   Nikuman _____ 50
   Pizzaman _____ 52
   Rice buns with shigureni _____ 80
   Uzumaki pan _____ 211
burdock root
   Rice buns with shigureni _____ 80
   shigureni (beef with ginger) _____ 80

C

cabbage
   Kalbi-don _____ 108
   Katsu sando _____ 160
   Mentai okonomiyaki _____ 142
   Morioka reimen _____ 144
   Okonomiyaki toast _____ 206
   Omu-yakisoba _____ 146
   Potato & beef croquettes _____ 61
   Shōga-yaki _____ 94
   Soy milk & pork nabe _____ 118
cakes
   Black sugar steamed cakes _____ 222
   Pound cake _____ 174
   Roll cake _____ 182
   the premium cake roll _____ 180
capsicums
   Kar pan (Curry buns) _____ 114
   Keema curry _____ 112
   Ketchup rice & spaghetti napolitan _____ 138
   Omu-yakisoba _____ 146
   Pizza toast _____ 204
caramel _____ 232, 234
carrots **14**
   Hashed beef _____ 104
   Hiyashi chūka _____ 136
   Hokkaido white stew _____ 98
   Karē pan (Curry buns) _____ 114
   Kashmir curry _____ 111
   Keema curry _____ 112
   Kiriboshi daikon _____ 124
   Makizushi _____ 34–7
   Omu-yakisoba _____ 146
   Soy milk & pork nabe _____ 118
   Sweet vinegar pickles _____ 126
   Wanpaku sando _____ 190
celery: Hokkaido white stew _____ 98
cheese
   cheese fried chicken _____ 72
   Croissant taiyaki _____ 237
   Fruit sando _____ 192
   Ham & cheese croquettes _____ 66
   ham & cheese French toast _____ 208
   Maritozzo _____ 178
   Mentai okonomiyaki _____ 142

Okonomiyaki toast _____ 206
Pizza toast _____ 204
Pizzaman _____ 52
Rice buns with shigureni _____ 80
Roll pizza _____ 82
Seafood gratin _____ 152–3
Steamed egg omelette sando _____ 188
Taiyaki _____ 236
Ume shiso chicken _____ 90
Wanpaku sando _____ 190
white sauce _____ 152
White taiyaki _____ 237
chicken
broth _____ 144
cheese fried chicken _____ 72
Chicken over rice _____ 134
Fried chicken _____ 70–2
Fried chicken bites _____ 74
Gochujang chicken onigiri _____ 29
Hokkaido white stew _____ 98
honey yuzu roast chicken _____ 78
Karaage _____ 76
Kashmir curry _____ 111
Morioka reimen _____ 144
Roast chicken _____ 78
Roll pizza _____ 82
Salad chicken _____ 244
spicy fried chicken _____ 72
Torimeshi onigiri _____ 26
Ume shiso chicken _____ 90
Wanpaku sando _____ 190
chillies
Kashmir curry _____ 111
Pork vindaloo _____ 116
Sardine peperoncino _____ 150
spice powder _____ 116
spicy fried chicken _____ 72
SEE ALSO gochujang, tobanjan
chirimen sansho onigiri _____ 23
chocolate
Choux cream puffs _____ 224
Custard cream _____ 237
Maritozzo _____ 178
Mochi donuts _____ 170
Uzumaki pan _____ 211
choux _____ 224
Choux cream puffs _____ 224
chūkaman
Chūkaman _____ 46
Gomaanman _____ 54
Nikuman _____ 50
Pizzaman _____ 52
coconut
marinade _____ 116
Pork vindaloo _____ 116
coffee
coffee jelly _____ 226
Coffee jelly parfait _____ 226
Coppe pan _____ 210
corn
batter _____ 176
Corn dog _____ 176
Potato salad _____ 123
Roll pizza _____ 82
Tuna mayo onigiri _____ 26
courgettes SEE zucchini
crabs _____ 246
Crab croquettes _____ 62
Kanimayo makizushi _____ 38
craquelin _____ 224

cream, Custard _____ 237
cream puffs, Choux _____ 224
Croissant taiyaki _____ 237
croquettes
Crab croquettes _____ 62
Ham & cheese croquettes _____ 66
Potato & beef croquettes _____ 61
Prawn croquettes _____ 64
crumbing _____ 62, 64, 66
cucumbers
Hiyashi chūka _____ 136
Makizushi _____ 34–7
Morioka reimen _____ 144
pickled cucumber _____ 123
Potato salad _____ 123
Sweet vinegar pickles _____ 126
curry
Karē pan (Curry buns) _____ 114
Kashmir curry _____ 111
Keema curry _____ 112
Pork vindaloo _____ 116
Custard cream _____ 237

D

daifuku _____ 228
Black sesame daifuku _____ 229
Soy milk daifuku _____ 229
Daigaku imo _____ 198
daikon _____ 246
Kalbi-don _____ 108
Kiriboshi daikon _____ 124
marinade _____ 108
Sanma kabayaki _____ 92
Soy milk & pork nabe _____ 118
Sweet vinegar pickles _____ 126
Dashi _____ 245
deep-freeze technology _____ 202
donuts
Mochi donuts _____ 170
Old-fashioned donuts _____ 172
Dorayaki _____ 230
doubanjiang SEE tobanjan
dough _____ 114
dressings _____ 123
miso sesame dressing _____ 124
Onion dressing _____ 126
dry coating _____ 70

E

Ebi chilli _____ 88
eggplant: Sardine peperoncino _____ 150
eggs
Black vinegar braised pork belly _____ 86
Choux cream puffs _____ 224
Croissant taiyaki _____ 237
crumbing _____ 62, 64, 66
Custard cream _____ 237
egg threads _____ 136
egg wash _____ 197, 211
Goya chanpuru _____ 121
ham & cheese French toast _____ 208
Hiyashi chūka _____ 136

Japanese French toast _____ 208
Kalbi-don _____ 108
Karē pan (Curry buns) _____ 114
Keema curry _____ 112
Morioka reimen _____ 144
Okonomiyaki toast _____ 206
omelette _____ 188
Omu-yakisoba _____ 146
Onsen eggs _____ 244
Purin _____ 232
Steamed egg omelette sando _____ 188
Taiyaki _____ 236
Tamago makizushi _____ 39
Tamago sando _____ 187
tartar sauce _____ 72
Wanpaku sando _____ 190
white sauce _____ 152
White taiyaki _____ 237
Yaki-purin _____ 234
ehōmaki _____ 34

F

Family Mart _____ 9, 33, 45, 70, 78
fish
chirimen sansho onigiri _____ 23
Sanma kabayaki _____ 92
Sardine peperoncino _____ 150
Seafood gratin _____ 152–3
SEE ALSO katsuobushi, roe, salmon, tuna
French toast, ham & cheese _____ 208
French toast, Japanese _____ 208
Fried chicken _____ 70–2
Fried chicken bites _____ 74
Fruit sando _____ 192
furikake onigiri _____ 23

G

ginger _____ 246
Black vinegar braised pork belly _____ 86
broth _____ 144
Ebi chilli _____ 88
Fried chicken _____ 70–2
Kalbi-don _____ 108
Karaage _____ 76
Karē pan (Curry buns) _____ 114
Kashmir curry _____ 111
Keema curry _____ 112
marinade _____ 108
marinade _____ 116
marinade _____ 76
Mentai okonomiyaki _____ 142
Morioka reimen _____ 144
Nikuman _____ 50
Okonomiyaki toast _____ 206
Pork vindaloo _____ 116
Rice buns with shigureni _____ 80
Roast chicken _____ 78
Salad chicken _____ 244
sauce _____ 94
shigureni (beef with ginger) _____ 80
Shōga-yaki _____ 94
Soy milk & pork nabe _____ 118

glaze _____ 197
glossary, ingredients _____ 246–7
glossary, Japanese _____ 130–3
gochujang
  broth _____ 144
  Gochujang chicken onigiri _____ 29
  Morioka reimen _____ 144
Gomaanman _____ 54
Goya chanpuru _____ 121
gratin, Seafood _____ 152–3

H

ham
  Croissant taiyaki _____ 237
  Ham & cheese croquettes _____ 66
  ham & cheese French toast _____ 208
  Hiyashi chūka _____ 136
  Ketchup rice & spaghetti napolitan _____ 138
  Omu-yakisoba _____ 146
  Pizza toast _____ 204
  Pizzaman _____ 52
  Potato salad _____ 123
  Roll pizza _____ 82
  Taiyaki _____ 236
  White taiyaki _____ 237
Hamburg steaks _____ 100
Hashed beef _____ 104
Hiyashi chūka _____ 136
Hokkaido white stew _____ 98
Hotcake mix _____ 166
Hotcakes _____ 168

I

Ikura/marinated salmon roe onigiri _____ 28
ingredient notes _____ 14
ingredients glossary _____ 246–7

J

Japanese French toast _____ 208
Japanese glossary _____ 130–3
jelly, coffee _____ 226

K

Kalbi-don _____ 108
Kanimayo makizushi _____ 38
Karaage _____ 76
Karaage-Kun _____ 69
Karē pan (Curry buns) _____ 114
Kashmir curry _____ 111
Katsu sando _____ 160
Katsudon _____ 160

katsuobushi
  Dashi _____ 245
  Goya chanpuru _____ 121
  Mentai okonomiyaki _____ 142
  Okaka (bonito flakes) onigiri _____ 25
  Okonomiyaki toast _____ 206
  Onion dressing _____ 126
Keema curry _____ 112
Ketchup rice & spaghetti napolitan _____ 138
Kiriboshi daikon _____ 124
kombu _____ **246**
  Dashi _____ 245
  Okaka (bonito flakes) onigiri _____ 25
  Soy milk & pork nabe _____ 118
  tsukudani onigiri _____ 23
konbini
  avatar-only operation _____ 201
  behind the konbini: a chat
    with Lawson _____ 215–17
  brand collaborations _____ 215–6
  deep-freeze technology _____ 202
  in the beginning _____ 33
  going local _____ 195
  konbini arenji _____ 96
  of the future _____ 201–2
  region specific _____ 217
  seasonal delights _____ 34, 42, 46, 215, 217
  social infrastructure _____ 107
  today _____ 57–8
  useful phrases _____ 130–3
  SEE ALSO 7-Eleven, Family Mart, Lawson
Kushiyaki _____ 97

L

Lawson _____ 9–10, 13,
  19, 23, 28, 33, 42, 45, 57–8, 69–70, 74,
  78, 107, 134, 180, 182, 186, 195, 201–2,
  215–17
  behind the konbini, a chat with Lawson
    215–17
  Green Lawson _____ 201, 216
  Lawson Farms _____ 58, 195, 217
  Natural Lawson _____ 216
  the Lawson premium roll cake _____ 180
leeks
  Omu-yakisoba _____ 146
  Prawn croquettes _____ 64
lemons
  Banana boats _____ 220
  Chicken over rice _____ 134
  Hokkaido white stew _____ 98
  Hotcakes _____ 168
  Lemon cream pasta _____ 140
  marinade _____ 134
  Onion dressing _____ 126
  Pound cake _____ 174
  white sauce _____ 134
limited-edition items _____ 215
lotus root: Pork vindaloo _____ 116

M

Makizushi _____ 34–7
marinades _____ 76, 108, 116, 134
Maritozzo _____ 178
Meatballs _____ 102
melon SEE bitter melon, watermelon
menchi katsu _____ 100
Mentai okonomiyaki _____ 142
mentaiko SEE roe
miso _____ **246**
  Awase miso onigiri _____ 29
  Blanched greens with miso
    sesame dressing _____ 124
  Kanimayo makizushi _____ 38
  Keema curry _____ 112
  Miso katsu _____ 157
  miso sesame dressing _____ 124
mochi
  black sesame mochi _____ 229
  Mentai okonomiyaki _____ 142
  Mochi donuts _____ 170
  mochipan _____ 210
  Soy milk daifuku _____ 229
  soy mochi _____ 229
Morioka reimen _____ 144
mushrooms
  Hashed beef _____ 104
  Ketchup rice
    & spaghetti napolitan _____ 138
  Nikuman _____ 50
  Seafood gratin _____ 152–3
  Soy milk & pork nabe _____ 118
  tsukudani onigiri _____ 23

N

nabe, Soy milk & pork _____ 118
Negi shio _____ 157
Negitoro makizushi _____ 38
Nikuman _____ 50
noodles
  Hiyashi chūka _____ 136
  Morioka reimen _____ 144
  Omu-yakisoba _____ 146
nori _____ **246**
  Awase miso onigiri _____ 29
  Gochujang chicken onigiri _____ 29
  Ikura/marinated salmon
    roe onigiri _____ 28
  Kanimayo makizushi _____ 38
  Makizushi _____ 34
  Negitoro makizushi _____ 38
  Okaka (bonito flakes) onigiri _____ 25
  Onigiri _____ 20–3
  Roll pizza _____ 82
  Shio salmon onigiri _____ 25
  Tamago makizushi _____ 39
  Torimeshi onigiri _____ 26
  Tuna mayo onigiri _____ 26
  Umeboshi onigiri _____ 28
nuts
  Kashmir curry _____ 111
  Maritozzo _____ 178

O

Okaka (bonito flakes) onigiri _____ 25
Okonomiyaki, Mentai _____ 142
Okonomiyaki toast _____ 206
Old-fashioned donuts _____ 172
omelette _____ 188
Omu-yakisoba _____ 146
omusubi SEE onigiri
onigiri
   a love story _____ 19
   Awase miso onigiri _____ 29
   chirimen sansho onigiri _____ 23
   furikake onigiri _____ 23
   Gochujang chicken onigiri _____ 29
   Ikura/marinated salmon roe onigiri _____ 28
   Okaka (bonito flakes) onigiri _____ 25
   Shio salmon onigiri _____ 25
   shiso & sesame onigiri _____ 23
   Torimeshi onigiri _____ 26
   tsukudani onigiri _____ 23
   Tuna mayo onigiri _____ 26
   Umeboshi onigiri _____ 28
   wakame onigiri _____ 23
   yukari onigiri _____ 23
Onion dressing _____ 126
Onsen eggs _____ 244

P

parfait, Coffee jelly _____ 226
pasta
   Ketchup rice & spaghetti napolitan _ 138
   Lemon cream pasta _____ 140
   Pasta with yamaimo & tarako _____ 148
   Sardine peperoncino _____ 150
   Seafood gratin _____ 152–3
pears
   Kalbi-don _____ 108
   marinade _____ 108
   Morioka reimen _____ 144
peas
   Hashed beef _____ 104
   Lemon cream pasta _____ 140
pickles
   amazu _____ 126
   pickled cucumber _____ 123
   Sweet vinegar pickles _____ 126
pies, Satsuma imo _____ 197
pizza, Roll _____ 82
Pizza toast _____ 204
Pizzaman _____ 52
plum
   Ume shiso chicken _____ 90
   SEE ALSO umeboshi
pork
   Black vinegar braised pork belly _____ 86
   Corn dog _____ 176
   Goya chanpuru _____ 121
   Hamburg steaks _____ 100
   Katsu sando _____ 160
   Katsudon _____ 160
   Meatballs _____ 102
   menchi katsu _____ 100
   Mentai okonomiyaki _____ 142

Nikuman _____ 50
Okonomiyaki toast _____ 206
Omu-yakisoba _____ 146
Pizza toast _____ 204
Pork vindaloo _____ 116
Shōga-yaki _____ 94
Soy milk & pork nabe _____ 118
Tonkatsu _____ 156
   SEE ALSO bacon, ham
potatoes _____ 14
   Ham & cheese croquettes _____ 66
   Hokkaido white stew _____ 98
   Potato & beef croquettes _____ 61
   Potato salad _____ 123
   Seafood gratin _____ 152–3
   SEE ALSO yamaimo
Pound cake _____ 174
prawns
   Ebi chilli _____ 88
   Prawn croquettes _____ 64
   Seafood gratin _____ 152–3
preferment _____ 184
Purin _____ 232

R

rice _____ **247**
   Awase miso onigiri _____ 29
   Chicken over rice _____ 134
   chirimen sansho onigiri _____ 23
   furikake onigiri _____ 23
   Gochujang chicken onigiri _____ 29
   Ikura/marinated salmon roe onigiri _____ 28
   Kanimayo makizushi _____ 38
   Ketchup rice & spaghetti napolitan _ 138
   Makizushi _____ 34
   Negitoro makizushi _____ 38
   Okaka (bonito flakes) onigiri _____ 25
   Rice buns with shigureni _____ 80
   Shio salmon onigiri _____ 25
   shiso & sesame onigiri _____ 23
   Tamago makizushi _____ 39
   Torimeshi onigiri _____ 26
   tsukudani onigiri _____ 23
   Tuna mayo onigiri _____ 26
   turmeric rice _____ 134
   Umeboshi onigiri _____ 28
   wakame onigiri _____ 23
   yukari onigiri _____ 23
Roast chicken _____ 78
roe _____ **246**
   Ikura/marinated salmon
      roe onigiri _____ 28
   Makizushi _____ 34–7
   Mentai okonomiyaki _____ 142
   Pasta with yamaimo & tarako _____ 148
   Roll pizza _____ 82
   Ume shiso chicken _____ 90
Roll cake _____ 182
Roll pizza _____ 82
roux _____ 98
rum
   Banana boats _____ 220
   rum sauce _____ 220
   Satsuma imo pies _____ 197

S

Salad chicken _____ 244
salad, Potato _____ 123
salmon
   Ikura/marinated salmon roe onigiri _____ 28
   Seafood gratin _____ 152–3
   Shio salmon onigiri _____ 25
sandos
   Fruit sando _____ 192
   Katsu sando _____ 160
   Steamed egg omelette sando _____ 188
   Tamago sando _____ 187
   Wanpaku sando _____ 190
Sanma kabayaki _____ 92
sansho
   chirimen sansho onigiri _____ 23
   honey yuzu roast chicken _____ 78
Sardine peperoncino _____ 150
Satsuma imo pies _____ 197
sauces _____ 94, 100, 102, 136
   Negi shio _____ 157
   rum sauce _____ 220
   tartar sauce _____ 72
   Tonkatsu sauce _____ 157
   white sauce _____ 134, 152
scallops
   Hokkaido white stew _____ 98
   Seafood gratin _____ 152–3
seasonal delights _____ 34, 42, 46, 215, 217
seasoning _____ 74
seaweed SEE aonori, kizami nori, kombu,
   nori, wakame
shigureni (beef with ginger) _____ 80
Shio salmon onigiri _____ 25
shiso _____ **247**
   Gochujang chicken onigiri _____ 29
   Makizushi _____ 34–7
   Pasta with yamaimo & tarako _____ 148
   shiso & sesame onigiri _____ 23
   Ume shiso chicken _____ 90
   yukari onigiri _____ 23
Shōga-yaki _____ 94
Shokupan _____ 184
skewers: Kushiyaki _____ 97
social infrastructure _____ 107
Soy milk & pork nabe _____ 118
Soy milk daifuku _____ 229
soy mochi _____ 229
spice blends
   seasoning _____ 74
   spice mix _____ 111, 112
   spice paste _____ 70
   spice powder _____ 116
spicy fried chicken _____ 72
spinach
   Blanched greens with miso
      sesame dressing _____ 124
   Makizushi _____ 34–7
   Seafood gratin _____ 152–3
spring onions
   Black vinegar braised pork belly _____ 86
   broth _____ 144
   Kalbi-don _____ 108
   Katsudon _____ 160
   marinade _____ 108
   Morioka reimen _____ 144
   Negi shio _____ 157

Negitoro makizushi _____ 38
Salad chicken _____ 244
Soy milk & pork nabe _____ 118
steak, Hamburg _____ 100
Steamed egg
   omelette sando _____ 188
stew, Hokkaido white _____ 98
stock: Dashi _____ 245
strawberries
Fruit sando _____ 192
Roll cake _____ 182
sushi
ehōmaki _____ 34
Kanimayo makizushi _____ 38
Makizushi _____ 34–37
Negitoro makizushi _____ 38
Tamago makizushi _____ 39
sweet potatoes _____ 196
Daigaku imo _____ 198
Satsuma imo pies _____ 197
sweet potato season _____ 195
Sweet vinegar pickles _____ 126

T

Taiyaki _____ 236
taiyaki, Croissant _____ 237
taiyaki, White _____ 237
Tamago makizushi _____ 39
Tamago sando _____ 187
tartar sauce _____ 72
toast
ham & cheese
   French toast _____ 208
Japanese French toast _____ 208
Okonomiyaki toast _____ 206
Pizza toast _____ 204
tobanjan _____ 247
Ebi chilli _____ 88
Kalbi-don _____ 108
marinade _____ 108
spicy fried chicken _____ 72
tofu
Fried chicken bites _____ 74
Goya chanpuru _____ 121
Kiriboshi daikon _____ 124
Mochi donuts _____ 170
tomatoes
Chicken over rice _____ 134
Hashed beef _____ 104
Hiyashi chka _____ 136
Karē pan (Curry buns) _____ 114
Kashmir curry _____ 111
Keema curry _____ 112
Pizzaman _____ 52
Pork vindaloo _____ 116
Rice buns
   with shigureni _____ 80
Roll pizza _____ 82
Sardine peperoncino _____ 150
Wanpaku sando _____ 190
Tonkatsu _____ 156
Tonkatsu sauce _____ 157
Torimeshi onigiri _____ 26
tsukudani onigiri _____ 23

tuna
Negitoro makizushi _____ 38
Roll pizza _____ 82
Tuna mayo onigiri _____ 26

U

umeboshi _____ **247**
Umeboshi onigiri _____ 28
Ume shiso chicken _____ 90
yukari onigiri _____ 23
Uzumaki pan _____ 211

W

waffles
Taiyaki _____ 236
White taiyaki _____ 237
Wanpaku sando _____ 190
watermelon: Morioka reimen _____ 144
white sauce _____ 134, 152
White taiyaki _____ 237
wine
Crab croquettes _____ 62
Hamburg steaks _____ 100
Hashed beef _____ 104
Hokkaido white stew _____ 98
Lemon cream pasta _____ 140
sauce _____ 100
Seafood gratin _____ 152–3

Y

Yaki-purin _____ 234
yamaimo _____ **247**
Pasta with yamaimo & tarako _____ 148
yukari onigiri _____ 23
yuzu: honey yuzu roast chicken _____ 78

Z

zucchini: Roll pizza _____ 82

Thanks

THIS BOOK WOULDN'T HAVE been possible without the trust of our publisher, Paul, who gave us the chance to dive off the deep end into a facet of Japanese culture well known but little covered. Thank you for giving us the chance to write about our obscure interest in konbinis! Thanks also to our editor Katri Hilden and recipe photography team Vicki Valsamis and Daniel Herrmann-Zoll.

Our deepest gratitude must also go to Mochimaru Ken-san of Lawson, Japan, who opened up the doors to Lawson and trusted us with writing their story. Little did we realise how fascinating this glimpse into the convenience store world would be. To Yuma, thank you for coming along, for your translation and for wanting Karaage-Kun as much as we did.

And finally, to Gorta Yuuki, our photographer – thank you for your patience, humour, and for going with our strange assignment. We love what you have done with the photography.

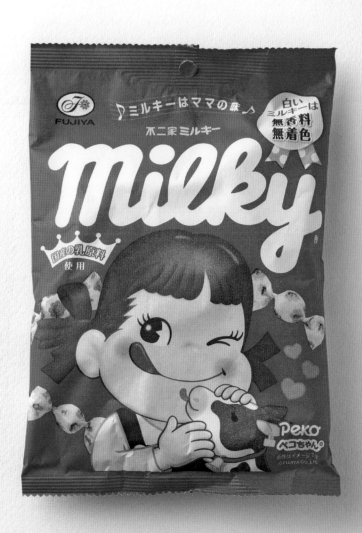

Published in 2024 by Smith Street Books
Naarm (Melbourne) | Australia
smithstreetbooks.com

ISBN: 978-1-9230-4931-4

Smith Street Books respectfully acknowledges the Wurundjeri People
of the Kulin Nation, who are the Traditional Owners of the land on which
we work, and we pay our respects to their Elders past and present.

Publisher: Paul McNally
Editor: Katri Hilden
Design and typesetting: Evi-O.Studio | Emi Chiba, Evi O
Location photography: Gorta Yuuki
Food photography: Daniel Herrmann-Zoll
Food styling: Vicki Valsamis
Food preparation: Brendan Liew
Proofreader: Pamela Dunne
Indexer: Helena Holmgren

Printed & bound in China by C&C Offset Printing Co., Ltd.

Book 344
10 9 8 7 6 5 4 3 2 1